LIFE'S ULTIMATE TO ~~DO~~ BE LIST

FINDING PURPOSE, GRACE, AND JOY IN A PERFORMANCE-DRIVEN WORLD

HONOR **H B** BOOKS

Inspiration and Motivation for the Seasons of Life

An Imprint of Cook Communications Ministries • Colorado Springs, CO

12 11 10 09 08 07 06 05   10 9 8 7 6 5 4 3 2 1

Life's Ultimate To ~~Do~~ Be List—Finding Purpose, Grace, and Joy in a Performance-Driven World
ISBN 1-56292-224-6

Copyright © 2005 by Bordon Books
6532 E. 71st Street, Suite 105
Tulsa, OK 74133

Published by Honor Books,
An Imprint of Cook Communications Ministries
4050 Lee Vance View
Colorado Springs, CO 80918
www.cookministries.com

Manuscript written by Killian Creative, Boulder, Colorado
Cover and interior designed by Jackson Design Co, Siloam Springs, AR

Introduction

From the time we begin school, we are encouraged to focus on achieving, performing, attaining, outdoing, impressing, and setting new standards of achievement and excellence. Although it may seem we are doing more in today's fast-paced society, performing better and achieving greater accomplishments than ever before, there is something missing. There has to be more to a "successful" life than performing well and accomplishing more and more while never attaining peace or experiencing depth of joy.

The Bible tells us there is wisdom in resting, in waiting, in letting go and relying on God. We are told not to lean on our own understanding but in all things to trust God is working for our good. It's not about how much we do or how far we go, it's about who we become. The race God has for us is a test of endurance based on character and commitment. To what degree we rest in Him, walk in love, show mercy and patient forbearance; are forgiving and faithful in the smallest details; are able to begin with the end—even eternity—in mind, ever relying on God's abundant grace, trusting, leaning, and abiding in the One who is the source of our strength and the author of all wisdom, to that degree we will find true and lasting success. May these meditations help you do that every day.

TODAY I WILL...

☑ trust God's plan for my life

☑ count my blessings

☑ be part of the good things to which God has called me

I KNOW WHAT I'M DOING. I HAVE IT ALL PLANNED
OUT—PLANS TO TAKE CARE OF YOU,
NOT ABANDON YOU, PLANS TO GIVE YOU THE
FUTURE YOU HOPE FOR.

JEREMIAH 29:11 MSG

The alarm rings after the third time you've hit snooze. The kids need to be woken up for school; the report you were working on until one o'clock last night for today's 10:00 A.M. meeting still needs a conclusion; and if you don't get up right now everyone will miss breakfast again. As it is, your options have already gone from eggs and toast to toaster strudel, so you drag yourself from bed, throw on a robe, yell down the hall for the kids to get up, and go brave the jungle of last night's dishes in search of the coffee machine. It appears it will be another chaotic day of busyness—rushing to get everything done before you crash your head back onto your pillow tonight.

You know what? God didn't create you because He wanted to be amused by someone struggling through their existence. God created you so that He could share the joy of living and the thrill of accomplishment with you. He created you for a unique purpose that would bring fulfillment to your life and to the lives of your loved ones—as well as bring a blessing to your world.

So how do you plug in to that? Perhaps the best way is to set your "To Do" list aside for a moment and pick up God's "To Be" list. If you are ready to get more out of life, this is a good place to start. Knowing God has a plan and calling for your life—a unique, divine, special, specific purpose—is the first step. As you sip your first cup of coffee this morning and you hear the first pattering of feet down the hallway, close your eyes for a moment and commit to God that if He will reveal His plan for your life, you will rise up to walk in it.

Remember, God never regrets the gifts and callings He has given us.

TODAY I WILL...

☑ be thankful for the challenge, exhilaration, and growth I gain from my job

☑ let my work fall into its proper place in the priorities of my day

☑ be a light for God's goodness wherever I am and whatever I do

---

IT IS A GOOD THING TO RECEIVE WEALTH FROM
GOD AND THE GOOD HEALTH TO ENJOY IT.
TO ENJOY YOUR WORK AND ACCEPT YOUR LOT IN
LIFE—THAT IS INDEED A GIFT FROM GOD.
ECCLESIASTES 5:19 NLT

Does it seem odd to think of your job as a gift from God or that good, hard work could be a blessing from the Lord?

Perhaps it does, but when the first Christians came to America to find the freedom to worship God as they felt led, their response to the issue of occupation and building wealth could be summed up in one word: "industry." In other words, they felt that being industrious in the time they had set aside to work would help them serve only God and not money. They saw their work—in its proper place—as a blessing and an act of worship. To become a workaholic was as bad as being lazy; there was always a point in the day to lay down your tools to spend time with your family and friends or to pray and fellowship with God.

We need to realize that good, challenging work that stretches us and makes us grow is indeed a gift from God. If the work we are doing now does not fit into that category, then perhaps it is time to start praying about it. Whatever areas of our lives we turn over to God, He will use them to build us up and conform us more to the image of His Son Jesus. The work we are called to is no different. Start letting God teach you from nine to five Monday through Friday, just as He does Sunday morning.

Remember, all things work for good if you love the Lord.

TODAY I WILL...

☑ be God's light in my workplace

☑ show God's love to my supervisors

☑ pray for and honor my leaders

LET EVERY SOUL BE SUBJECT
UNTO THE HIGHER POWERS.
FOR THERE IS NO POWER BUT OF GOD:
THE POWERS THAT BE ARE ORDAINED OF GOD.

ROMANS 13:1 KJV

God called David a man after His own heart, but David was far from perfect. One of the things that set David as a Godly example to us, though, was his attitude towards King Saul. Saul was in the wrong and sought to hurt David in any way that he could, but David refused to rebel against the man God had called to lead Israel. Even though David had chances to end Saul's life on at least two occasions, he refused to harm the one God had called to be his king. In the one instance, he cut Saul's robe to show him that he had been there and could have hurt Saul, but did not; later he repented before God for the disrespect he had shown the anointed king of God's people. (See 1 Samuel 24:3-12.)

Submitting to people whom we don't necessarily agree with can be a pretty taxing experience. Imagine what it was like for David as he holed up in one cave after another trying to stay out of Saul's way. In contrast, it seems unlikely that any of us really have it that bad. However, if we will stand firm in our faith in God, just as David did, God will see us through. Don't forget that, despite his hardships, David also went on to be one of the greatest writers of God's praise in Bible history. That is because he looked to God alone for his salvation.

Remember, promotion comes from the Lord.

TODAY I WILL...

☑ be a nurturing influence to those around me

☑ put aside my agenda and be present for those God brings across my path

☑ take time to listen

"I TELL YOU THE TRUTH, WHATEVER YOU DID FOR ONE OF THE LEAST OF THESE BROTHERS OF MINE, YOU DID FOR ME."

MATTHEW 25:40 NIV

Too often our plans take precedence over people—our personal agendas distract us from the quiet suffering, hopes, and dreams of those around us. In our program-driven world, we forget that the kingdom of God is shared one heart at a time—one loving word, selfless deed, or kind gesture that can give someone a glimpse of the hope we have because of Jesus.

More can be accomplished by a willing ear during a few minutes of mindful attention—a momentary connection extended to meet the need of a searching soul—than by the most organized, publicized, and subsidized evangelistic campaigns. When someone asks if you have a moment to talk today, take the time to not only listen, but genuinely hear. Even if the conversation appears to be only about a mundane subject or office project, realize there may be a deeper need that person is searching to meet.

If we are willing, God will give us a word for the weary—the right word at the right time—a liberating, healing word just when someone needs it most. It is through the Godly words we speak that change can come into our everyday lives. It is the attention that we are willing to render that brings hope to a hurried, inattentive, and careless world.

Remember, every encounter with another is an opportunity to see God at work.

TODAY I WILL...

☑ be faithful in the little things

☑ look for God's hand at work in the smallest details

☑ appreciate the nuances of my work, hopes, and goals

HE THAT IS FAITHFUL IN THAT WHICH IS
LEAST IS FAITHFUL ALSO IN MUCH.

LUKE 16:10 KJV

Maybe we can't control the cost of gas, rising interest rates, or falling stock prices, but we can bring some order to the chaos of modern life by staying attentive to the smaller details of living. We can de-clutter our hearts by acknowledging God in everything we do—by being faithful in the very little things of our lives, beginning with every thought we think and every word we speak.

We are commanded to rejoice and be thankful at all times for all things, even the very smallest things. God's creation is majestic in its detailed perfection. God is almighty because He cares about your deepest desires and innermost thoughts. God is a God of the smallest detail.

Don't neglect the small things. Give attention to the details. Be mindful of the process and honor the journey. It is in esteeming the mundane that we give glory to the Majestic.

Remember, details count.

Today I Will...

☑ be led by love

☑ take God's peace everywhere
I go

☑ look for opportunities to be a
blessing

Let us not grow weary
while doing good.

Galatians 6:9 nkjv

Most of us are much too busy to add anything more to our already overextended schedules. We cringe at thoughts of taking on additional obligations. We have our hands full with personal responsibilities and the daily demands of our jobs, homes, and family activities. We are ordinary people with limited time and finite abilities.

Yet all of us have experienced the exhilaration of being at the right place at the right time to bless someone unexpectedly. Being "prepared for every good work" does not necessarily require a financial investment or additional time commitment, but a willing heart. The "preparation of the gospel of peace" that Paul speaks of in Ephesians is more of an attitude than a skill. Are we willing vessels, yielded to the leadings and promptings of the Holy Spirit?

The joy of doing the gospel comes from allowing God's love to be available through us. To "be prepared" is simply to be available—attentive and mindful of those precious moments when a spontaneous kindness can illuminate a soul, bringing God's ever-abundant peace, joy, and light.

Remember, God is love.

TODAY I WILL...

- ☑ remember that God is at work in every situation
- ☑ choose optimism over pessimism
- ☑ lean not on my own understanding

WE KNOW THAT IN ALL THINGS GOD WORKS
FOR THE GOOD OF THOSE WHO LOVE HIM,
WHO HAVE BEEN CALLED ACCORDING TO
HIS PURPOSE.

ROMANS 8:28 NIV

It seems human nature to panic. Who doesn't sometimes expect the worst or keep expectations at a minimum? We all lie awake at night dwelling on the "what if's?" and the "how so's" or "how in the world's?" and sometimes the "God help me's."

Often it is all we can do to remember that the steps of God's children are ordered by Him—that God is working the good in every situation on behalf of those who love Him. We don't need to be anxious because we know that God is watching over us carefully and affectionately. We can let go of our concerns about how quickly we are reaching our destination and simply enjoy the journey.

If we are truly trusting in God, it is up to us to surrender control and let God carry us over life's rapids and rough places. Resting in Him can be the most difficult challenge. Determine to let the peace of God rule in your heart and mind. Purpose to rest in God's perfect peace.

Remember, God is at work in every situation fulfilling His plan for you.

TODAY I WILL...

☑ start with the end in mind

☑ live for eternity, not the tyranny of the urgent or the attraction of the temporary

☑ pray for vision to see the big picture

THERE'S FAR MORE HERE THAN MEETS THE EYE.
THE THINGS WE SEE NOW ARE HERE TODAY,
GONE TOMORROW. BUT THE THINGS WE CAN'T SEE
NOW WILL LAST FOREVER.

2 CORINTHIANS 4:18 MSG

You've crossed another "to do" from your list, accomplished another task, fulfilled another function on your job description—but have you stopped to ask yourself, "Just why, exactly, am I doing this?"

For most of us, there was a time when getting a job and earning a paycheck was enough. The rent was covered, the cable bill was paid, and there was food in the refrigerator for the weekend. But after awhile, is it still enough? What attracted you to your work in the first place? Why is it you show up each day and spend most of your energy doing what you do?

We can be busy all day long fulfilling others' expectations while never getting closer to realizing our God-given potential. People who work primarily for a paycheck will prioritize their schedules, but people of purpose schedule their priorities. Are you exercising your freedom of choice? How is what you are doing getting you closer to becoming who God created you to be?

*Remember, how you choose
to be today will determine where
you'll be tomorrow.*

TODAY I WILL...

☑ touch the lives of others in a positive way

☑ reevaluate the quality of my relationships with others

☑ take the time to be polite and courteous despite the pressures of the tasks before me

EACH PART GETS ITS MEANING FROM THE BODY AS A WHOLE, NOT THE OTHER WAY AROUND.

ROMANS 12:4 MSG

In the business world of modern, independence-minded America, we hear a lot about the importance of teamwork. Yet at the same time our culture and media honor heroes who stand out. It is not the whole team that gets their picture on the cover of magazines and newspapers, but the MVP athlete, most vocal government official, company president, the best-looking actor of the hit film or popular TV series. While it is the team that really accomplishes something, it is the stars who are recognized. Thus the pressure on the individual is to be the star rather than the team player, and this pressure often works to undermine the efforts of the team to accomplish anything worthwhile.

The star mentality teaches us that we are defined by our achievements. However, the Bible tells us that we would more correctly evaluate ourselves by the quality of our relationships. Do we walk in love toward other members of the team? Do we exemplify the fruit of the Spirit when around them? (See Galatians 5:22.) Do we value them more than promotion and the money it might bring? Do we lord authority over them, or are we servant-leaders as Jesus exemplified?

The truth of the matter is that God has wired us to need each other. Without feedback from and interaction with others, we would never truly grow spiritually. While we might grow in knowledge of God in isolation, we could never grow in the practice of His principles and power. Seek to make relationships your focus today.

Remember, faith without practical application is worthless and lifeless.

TODAY I WILL...

☑ remember that it all begins and ends with God

☑ entrust my life to the One who gives me breath and has the power to change my heart

☑ ask God where He wants me to spend my time and invite Him into the circumstances and relationships of my day

THE STEPS OF THE GODLY ARE DIRECTED BY THE LORD. HE DELIGHTS IN EVERY DETAIL OF THEIR LIVES.

PSALM 37:23 NLT

What do you do when things don't turn out as you have planned? What happens when the one big thing that you had to get accomplished today doesn't get done because something else came up? Does it mean that your plans were worthless or misguided in some way?

Such occurrences always give us a place to sit back and reevaluate. The answers to these questions, however, may have more to do with our attitudes than with the quality of our planning. The question is, are we dedicating our plans to God or allowing God to alter our plans to touch someone or teach us something new? Could it be that for an hour, a day, a week, or even a year, God might have something more important for us to accomplish than just ticking off more steps towards the fulfillment of our goals?

If our lives are dedicated to God, then we need to realize that there are times He needs to intervene to get us back on the right track—His track. Joseph dreamt that his brothers would bow down to him (Genesis 37:5-7,9), but had he not been sold into slavery, gone to prison because of a false accusation, and spent years seeking God rather than seeking the fulfillment of his God-given dreams, then he would never have been a person worthy of his brothers' respect and admiration. God cares more about who we become than what we accomplish.

Remember, God is
the Source of your life.

TODAY I WILL...

☑ allow the Word of God to govern my thought life

☑ take every thought captive

☑ think like Christ

WE ARE DESTROYING SPECULATIONS AND EVERY
LOFTY THING RAISED UP AGAINST THE KNOWLEDGE
OF GOD, AND WE ARE TAKING EVERY THOUGHT
CAPTIVE TO THE OBEDIENCE OF CHRIST.

2 CORINTHIANS 10:5 NASB

Ordering our thoughts by guarding our minds against ungodly imaginations is our first defense against the schemes of the enemy. The battle for our hearts and minds takes place in our thought life. We must purpose to think thoughts pleasing to God, filling our minds with scriptures declaring the promises of God.

In putting on the full armor that Paul speaks of in Ephesians 6, we must wear truth like a belt around our minds. Peter makes reference to the same concept in his instruction to "gird up the loins of your mind." After girding our loins with the belt of truth, we are told to put on the breastplate of righteousness. A breastplate is something that guards the heart. We can use the righteousness of God to guard our hearts by remembering we've been made the righteousness of God in Christ. (See 2 Corinthians 5:21.) The enemy will do all he can to cause you to believe you are a failure, unworthy, and unacceptable in the sight of God. The truth (His Word), however, states otherwise.

In order to effectively wear the armor of God, we must continually be mindful of God, His Word, and His Holy Spirit at work in us. If we are girded about with the belt of truth, guarded by the breastplate of righteousness, shod with the preparation of the gospel of peace, surrounded by the shield of faith, protected by the helmet of salvation, and wielding the sword of the Spirit, we will certainly be in pursuit of God's presence and in a position to be led by His Spirit.

*Remember, in pursuing God
we must choose to put on His armor,
not our own.*

TODAY I WILL...

☑ choose my words wisely

☑ speak truthfully in love

☑ seek the feedback I need to make me a better person and do my job more effectively

THE RIGHT WORD AT THE RIGHT TIME IS LIKE A CUSTOM-MADE PIECE OF JEWELRY, AND A WISE FRIEND'S TIMELY REPRIMAND IS LIKE A GOLD RING SLIPPED ON YOUR FINGER.

PROVERBS 25:11-12 MSG

The power of the right words or the right idea at the appropriate time is immeasurable. David's words to Saul as Goliath marched back and forth mocking Israel snatched victory from the mouth of cowardice. (See 1 Samuel 17:33-37.) Nathan's timely rebuke in the form of the parable of the rich man stealing the only lamb of a poor man brought King David repentantly back to God (2 Samuel 12:1-13), keeping him the man after God's own heart and correcting the course of Israel for a generation or more.

The right words can inspire, redirect, and empower. However, the timing is often as important as the choice of thoughts and ideas to convey, and discerning that timing and that choice of words can be difficult. In fact, there are even times when the best thing to do is to hold your peace. As the Bible aptly points out, "Even a fool is thought wise if he keeps silent, and discerning if he holds his tongue" (Proverbs 17:28 NIV).

As you pray today, ask God to help you keep guard over what you say, when you say it, and even if you should say anything at all. Determine in your heart that whatever comes out of your mouth will be to encourage and build others up, and not to appease your desire to feel superior or escalate yourself. Seek to operate as Jesus did: "I do nothing on my own authority, but I say only what the Father has instructed me to say" (John 8:28 TEV).

Remember, if you fill your heart with the right things, that is what you will speak of the most. (See Matthew 12:34.)

TODAY I WILL...

☑ walk in the joy of knowing God

☑ experience the wonder
of the world around me

☑ rejoice in the mundane

REJOICE IN THE LORD ALWAYS:
AND AGAIN I SAY, REJOICE.

PHILIPPIANS 4:4 KJV

The smell of coffee. The warmth of a shower. The feel of clean teeth. When was the last time you stopped and acknowledged the beauty of a sunrise, a tree, or a child? Relished the sensation of breathing, seeing, or tasting?

We can feel so impoverished by the disappointments and demands of life, while at the same time we are offered a rich abundance of small, often-unappreciated moments of beauty and joy. Don't let the seemingly oppressive cares of this world darken the hope you have in Christ.

Purpose to fully appreciate the intricate wonder you find in the world around you. Expect to experience the profound depth of meaning God has woven into every moment, perspective, and conclusion you uncover in all you dare to witness—knowing that in Him we live, move, and have our being.

We have no shortage
of opportunities to rejoice
in our Creator.

Today I Will...

☑ walk confident of my Savior's presence

☑ listen for His voice

☑ trust His ways and His guidance in my heart

In God I have put my trust;
I will not be afraid.

Psalm 56:11 nkjv

What would it really be like to have Jesus walk with us physically everywhere we go? What would we do differently? How would we behave? Or would we just let Him lead the way?

If we truly trust God and His words to us from the Bible, then one of the ways that we can strengthen that trust is to take to heart the fact that He is with us and will never forsake us. If Jesus is truly at our side—as well as on our side—do we really have to strive so hard to get ahead? Would we really worry so much about meeting deadlines? Would we let the stress of daily life get the best of us to the point that we cause others stress rather than help ease their burdens?

God's promises aren't just for when we are with other Christians. God wants us to know Him and feel His presence with us every day and in every place of our lives. He wants us to have success in every area of our lives by trusting in Him and walking in His ways. Take several opportunities today to stop and think of what it would be like if Jesus were literally standing right next to you at that moment—because, in truth, He is right there waiting for you to acknowledge Him.

Remember, God always wants what is best for you.

TODAY I WILL...

☑ remember that God's joy is my strength

☑ be a source of peace, encouragement, and steadiness in a stressful and frequently belittling world

☑ know that the answer to tough times often lies in just getting through them

EVEN WHEN I WALK THROUGH THE DARK VALLEY OF DEATH, I WILL NOT BE AFRAID, FOR YOU ARE CLOSE BESIDE ME.

PSALM 23:4 NLT

Jesus once told the story of two builders: one who built his house on unstable, shifting sand; and the other who built his home on a foundation of solid rock. (See Matthew 7:24-27.) In the story a storm arose and hit both houses. Neither builder had a hope of avoiding the storm. However, at the end of it, the house on the rock still stood, even if slightly weather-beaten and in need of some small repairs. The other, however, had washed away, and nothing could be found of it but rubble.

We often forget that the tough times of this world can come upon us all—that following Jesus is not a promise of smooth sailing on continually sunny seas. We forget that the issue is not necessarily avoiding the storms, but getting safely to the other side. Many times that means making sure we have solidly founded our endeavors on Godly principles rather than on selfish desires. We must make sure we are not getting ourselves so lost in the details of life that we are blown this way or that with no fixed course through life.

In the midst of the storm, there is often little we can do but hang on and ride it out. However, it is also good to know that the One who calmed the seas is with us and by our sides to see us through. Pull on His strength to stand firm in your faith no matter how the circumstances appear.

Remember, He promised to never leave you nor forsake you. (See Hebrews 13:5.)

Today I Will...

- ☑ earnestly seek the truth in every situation
- ☑ be honest in all I communicate to others
- ☑ let only things that honor God come out of my mouth

God cares about honesty in the workplace; your business is his business.

Proverbs 16:11 msg

With the constant pressure on many of us to produce fast results, generate short-term profits, or find quick answers for our supervisors, it seems we are under constant pressure to cut corners to get ahead. Cutting little corners now, however, often leads to blatant cuts across the middle of the track later. Remember, Jesus told us that those who would be unfaithful in little would also be unfaithful in much. (See Luke 16:10.) Honesty and integrity start wherever you are today.

Our greatest tests of faith in God's ways often come when no one else is looking. The cookie jar is no temptation if Mom is standing in the room, but the moment she leaves, its appeal can seem overwhelming—even if reaching it means scaling to the top of the refrigerator. How we use our time at work, how thoroughly we research our reports, how we speak to and relate with our fellow employees and customers, and how diligently we apply ourselves to whatever task is before us are all reflections of how much we really believe—or don't believe—God's ways are better.

It is also good to know, though, that God is constantly there with us to make up the difference and help us out if doing things His way seems to put us behind. God will not fail to honor us if we honor and walk with Him.

Remember, God's ways are higher than our ways.

TODAY I WILL...

☑ find joy and satisfaction in doing my best

☑ appreciate the beauty of a job well done

☑ see God's grace in what He has called me to do at work, at home, and wherever I give my time

LOVE NEVER FAILS.

1 CORINTHIANS 13:8 NIV

Do you love what you do?

That may not be such an easy question to answer sometimes. Maybe you started your career with purpose, or perhaps circumstances just seemed to lead you to the place you are now. Your "career" may be in an office, a business, or being the "Human Resources Director" for your own family. Whatever the case, how much love you put into any job often determines how much satisfaction you get out of it—as well as whether or not the job is done with excellence. Nothing can sap life out of us as much as just going through the motions each day to accomplish the tasks at hand without conscientious involvement. If we do that too long, we begin to feel more like machines than people, and our sense of divine purpose gets lost in monotony.

However, nothing we do should be ordinary or boring. We have an intangible element within us that gives life to whatever we do. It is the love of God that He has poured generously into our hearts. Letting that love shine out of us no matter how mundane the task can prove to be the difference between the rich man's gifts and the widow's two mites.

With God's Spirit within us and His love flowing out of us, nothing should be ordinary or boring.

Remember, the more of His love that we pour into our world, the more of His love God can pour into our lives.

TODAY I WILL...

☑ strive to see my work the way God sees it

☑ live for God's purposes and grace rather than just being busy

☑ focus on what really needs to be accomplished and not let unimportant, unfinished business rob me of time and energy better spent with my loved ones

---

THE ASPIRATIONS OF GOOD PEOPLE
END IN CELEBRATION; THE AMBITIONS OF
BAD PEOPLE CRASH.

PROVERBS 10:28 MSG

It is the nature of God within us that drives us to create and achieve. However, what we create and achieve we often let circumstances determine for us. Paul tells Timothy in 2 Timothy 1:9 that God did not call us because of the works we would do, but according to His purposes and grace. If we don't submit our aspirations to Him consciously, we can too often fill up our days with busyness, anxiety, and activity, but really accomplish nothing worthwhile.

People who can focus on the important and accomplish it each day have better control of their time and feel better about themselves. Those who show up at work and just start answering the phone, responding to any e-mails that pop up on their computers, or get lost in the myriad of little things that should be done, but can wait, will often find they are leaving at the end of the day with nothing having really been accomplished. A little advanced planning can keep such daily, urgent demands at bay.

Start with prayer and ask God to help you organize your day. Look at all you have to do and dedicate blocks of time to work on the important things first. Set aside time when you are freshest and most alert for the things that are most significant. Then don't just plan your business day, but think about what you might do with your loved ones tonight that would help them see how really important they are to you as well.

Remember, God knows why He put you on the earth and will give you the strength and vision to accomplish it if you will let Him.

Today I Will...

☑ look for serenity in the currents of my day

☑ create pockets of God's peace

☑ not rage with any storms that may come my way

"Blessed is the man who trusts me, God, the woman who sticks with God. They're like trees replanted in Eden, putting down roots near the rivers—never a worry through the hottest of summers, never dropping a leaf, serene and calm through droughts, bearing fresh fruit every season."

Jeremiah 17:7-8 msg

The Hebrew term for "peace"—shalom—is a powerful concept if we can get ahold of it for our lives. For many, peace means simply the absence of conflict and strife, which is a good thing; but the concept of shalom goes beyond that definition to mean not only lack of conflict, but also an active element of goodwill—not only will I not attack you, but as far as is within my power, I will also be a blessing to you.

In any workplace, crises are not uncommon. In fact, most businesses face them on a regular basis, if not as a normal part of their day. Deadlines, production schedules, meetings, changes in the marketplace, or any number of demands can lead to a need to "get things done NOW!" Even worse are the dreaded words: "We are going to have to stay until this is done."

For those who trust in God, however, there is no need for anxiety in the midst of any storm. We know that we will make it safely to the other side. Yet even if we are under attack in the midst of the situation—our supervisor dumps his or her stress on us, or everyone is running around and short-tempered—do we have to do the same? Or can we radiate blessings while others can do nothing but curse? Those who trust in the Lord—whether in times of high heat or barren periods of drought—can still bear good fruit if their roots run deep in God's goodness and love.

Remember, God has put you where you are to be a blessing.

Today I Will...

☑ treat others with the respect due to them by God, rather than their positions or authority

☑ seek to reach out to people who need a helping hand

☑ see people as God sees them

"Whenever you did one of these things to someone overlooked or ignored, that was me—you did it to me."

Matthew 25:40 msg

Wisdom dictates that those things that last the longest are deserving of the most attention. Your company or business won't make it into eternity, but the people you touch through it might. How much more important is it then to value those you work for—or those who work for you—than it is to use them to get ahead? Ten thousand years from now, what will be the more valuable investment?

Our human nature and culture have indirectly taught us that the easiest way to build ourselves up is to tear others down. Rather than working to grow ourselves, or even investing in others to help them grow, we are too often satisfied to simply reduce everyone to the lowest common denominator for the sake of feeling adequate. Such attitudes, however, can unravel a great deal of good. As Ecclesiastes 10:1 says, "Dead flies putrefy the perfumer's ointment, and cause it to give off a foul odor; so does a little folly to one respected for wisdom and honor."

In the parable of the sheep and the goats (Matthew 25:31-46), Jesus stated that the only way to physically bless Him was to physically meet the needs of others—even the least of them. If this principle is true, then not only does our charity matter, but so does our treatment of others in the workplace. Perhaps we need to go beyond the question of "What would Jesus do?" to ask "If the person in the cubicle next to me were Jesus, what would I do?"

Remember, God is
no respecter of persons.

TODAY I WILL...

☑ go to work as I would go to church

☑ seek opportunities to bless in the smallest of ways

☑ worship God with my work habits and the way I interact with others

LIVE WISELY AMONG THOSE WHO ARE NOT CHRISTIANS, AND MAKE THE MOST OF EVERY OPPORTUNITY.

COLOSSIANS 4:5 NLT

Have you ever thought about entering the office where you work as a place where you plan to praise God, learn something new to apply to your pursuit of God, and touch others with His love?

Certainly we have heard that we should be living in God's presence more than just at our church services on Sundays, but how do we take being with God beyond our weekly worship? How do we experience Him at work when we are normally too busy to even remember we are Christians, let alone take a moment to stop and sing a song of praise to God?

Perhaps, however, singing and thanking God verbally are not the only ways to praise Him. In fact, Psalm 50:23 MSG says, "It's the praising life that honors me." As the old saying goes, "Actions speak louder than words." Can we praise God louder by walking in His ways Monday through Friday than we can by exclaiming the wonder of His ways with all our hearts Sunday mornings?

Some of the greatest opportunities to share our faith start with someone else coming up to us and saying, "You know, there is something different about you. What is it?" Praise God today by letting His love shine through you in everything that you do.

Remember, the strength of our words comes from how well our lifestyle backs them up.

Today I Will...

- ☑ love the process and routine of my work

- ☑ look for opportunity in crisis

- ☑ take responsibility when others are looking to hide or blame

"You're blessed when you feel you've lost what is most dear to you. Only then can you be embraced by the One most dear to you."

Matthew 5:4 msg

We have all been brought up to dislike failure—however, there have been few who have risen to their greatest achievements without tasting it and using it as a springboard to triumph. In Romans 8:37, Paul called us "more than conquerors." How can one become a conqueror without something to overcome?

Jesus gave us the ultimate example of being a conqueror: Though He walked perfectly on the earth, He still faced and embraced the Cross for what would be gained through it. What would be gained? A sinful world—a world full of failures, if you will—would find forgiveness and redemption from their failures. Were the failures of the world Jesus' fault? We can answer only with a resounding, "No!" However, despite the fact that He was not at fault, He still spread His arms wide and said, "I will take responsibility and pay the price for their mistakes."

It is only those who take responsibility—even for problems they did not cause—who will ultimately provide the solution that will turn apparent defeat and failure into victory. Will you be available today to be part of the solution rather than contributing to the problem?

Remember, Jesus has the answer to whatever question you may ask.

Today I Will...

☑ esteem the time I invest in my activities

☑ ask for God's guidance in determining the best way to prioritize my schedule

☑ be an example of God's wisdom to those around me and my loved ones in my work habits and the way I spend my free time

Be careful how you walk, not as unwise men but as wise, making the most of your time, because the days are evil.

Ephesians 5:15-16 nasb

Far too often we underestimate the most valuable commodity we have been given so freely once we are born—the irreplaceable gift of time. Think about it for a moment: If we lose money, we can always work or invest to replace it; lost time, however, is gone forever. Yet, while it seems that advice about investing money abounds, when is the last time you saw a television commercial for someone offering to help you invest your time?

It has been said more than once that there are basically three things that we can invest for a return or give to help others: our time, our talents, and our treasure. Of these three, time is the most precious. In fact, all of us who work at a job are actually trading our time and talent for a paycheck. Those who build companies from the ground up and those who spend their lives working for minimum wage both have the same amount of time, but they've chosen to invest it in different ways.

Only a foolish person would invest something without hoping that it would provide a return of some sort, whether that return be for themselves or for someone else. What are you investing your time in today? Who will benefit from it? As you make out your schedule today—both for work and home—take a minute to ask yourself what you are investing in and who will benefit. What can you do to improve the return on your time investments?

Remember, you will reap the harvest of the "seeds" you sow.

Today I Will...

☑ look for opportunities to give into the lives of others

☑ be part of the cycle of blessing

☑ be a blessing to those whose messages bless me and whom I believe in

My God will fully supply your every need according to his glorious riches in Christ Jesus.

Philippians 4:19 isv

Paul prayed this blessing over the offering he had received from the Philippians while he was in prison in Rome. Their offering to him came as a sweet-smelling sacrifice to the Lord and also symbolized their continued dedication to what they had learned from Paul even though he was now in prison for it. For this, Paul prayed that God would fully supply their need because of their generosity—in essence, that God's generosity would be poured out on them because they had so willingly poured out blessings on him. A cycle of blessing was formed because they gave out of their hearts and their pocketbooks to help Paul when he was in need.

The same cycle of blessing exists in the church today as we give into our local churches and to ministry and missionary organizations as God leads us. Even non-Christians who have written financial books recognize the importance of giving and entering into the cycle of blessing that comes from having a generous heart.

Many have been mistaken, however, because they have assumed that the blessing of the money they give would come back to them in the same way it went out—that God would have someone write them a check just as He had them write a check to sow to someone else. However, as businesspeople and entrepreneurs, we should look for much more than that. We should expect God to bless us with new ideas and technologies to sustain our businesses to produce more for us to give down the road. Our businesses and employment are blessed just as we are a blessing.

Remember, it is more blessed to give than to receive. (See Acts 20:35.)

TODAY I WILL...

☑ watch my temper

☑ try to understand where others are coming from

☑ choose my words to produce healing and nurturing rather than abrasion

LOVE ISN'T SELFISH OR QUICK TEMPERED.

1 CORINTHIANS 13:5 CEV

Very often little things that bother us in the lives of others are problems we are blind to in our own lives. In the Sermon on the Mount, Jesus asked, "How can you think of saying, 'Let me help you get rid of that speck in your eye,' when you can't see past the log in your own eye?'" (Matthew 7:4 NLT). If we would heed Jesus' words in this instance, then we should pay attention to our pet peeves and use them as a place to begin examining our own ways.

The quickest—often automatic—form of judging others is actually anger. When do we get angry? We might say it's when we are offended, when we feel unjustly treated, or when something doesn't seem fair to us. We actually get angry because somehow our self-image has been challenged or our core motives have been hampered. In other words, we get angry because someone has interfered with what we want or threatened our position or authority. How often do such outbursts begin in our minds with, "Well! Just who do they think they are?" when perhaps the better question might be, "Just who do I think I am?"

Even if I am the CEO of my company, I need to realize that the CEO of life itself said, "Whatever measure you use in judging others . . . will be used to measure how you are judged" (Matthew 7:2 NLT). Perhaps when anger rises to the surface, we would be better off asking ourselves why we are getting angry rather than releasing that anger on someone else. Most likely, we won't have a more honest "time to remove the log in our eye" indicator than that!

Remember, The fruit of righteousness will be peace; the effect of righteousness will be quietness and confidence forever. (Isaiah 32:17 NIV)

TODAY I WILL...

☑ celebrate the triumphs of others

☑ look for opportunities to acknowledge contributions that would otherwise go unnoticed

☑ use my influence to encourage and lift up

[LOVE] DOESN'T REVEL WHEN OTHERS GROVEL,
[IT] TAKES PLEASURE IN THE FLOWERING OF
TRUTH.

1 CORINTHIANS 13:6 MSG

There is a commodity in the workplace that many think money and authority follow: credit for a job well done. In fact, this commodity is so coveted that it is stolen more often than money. It seems every employee wants to be able to stand before their supervisor and say, "I was responsible for that"—whether it is true or not.

It seems obvious that if we are to walk in God's way, we must see that credit is given to those to whom it is due. Yet, as with many things, living by this principle is easier said than done. No matter how much teamwork may be preached as a company value, advancement is still based upon competition. To advance, we have to show we are better qualified than our coworkers. When a supervisor pats us on the back, it takes much more effort to let them know who really was responsible rather than just accepting the compliment with a smile and a thank you. Giving the impression that you were responsible for something that was only partially a result of your efforts is the same as lying. Besides, those who get ahead by taking credit for the accomplishments of others rarely stay ahead in the long run.

It is not where you are in the middle of the race that counts, but how you finish. In the midst of that race, while others may be doing whatever they can to get ahead, those who truly believe that promotion comes from the Lord (Psalm 75:6-7) will operate differently. Those whose hope is in the Lord will take pleasure in the truth because they know He is the One from whom true promotion comes.

Remember, it is amazing what can be accomplished when no one cares who gets the credit.

TODAY I WILL...

☑ look beyond today's limitations to embrace what might be

☑ remember what first inspired me in the work I am now doing

☑ never, never, never give up hope

[LOVE] BEARS UP UNDER EVERYTHING, BELIEVES THE BEST IN ALL, THERE IS NO LIMIT TO HER HOPE, AND NEVER WILL SHE FALL.

1 CORINTHIANS 13:7 ISV

Hope is one of the most valuable commodities on earth. Without it we can do nothing. Hope is the doorway through which faith comes into our lives and whose hinges are lubricated by the love of God that we let flow through us. If that door has rusted shut because our love has "dried up," then hope will be "shut up," and the faith we need to move forward and accomplish our dreams will be "shut out."

The Bible tells us though that God's love has been liberally poured into our hearts (see Romans 5:5). In any situation that seems hopeless, tapping into that love is the key to getting the door of hope open again. When we love what we do and let God's love reach out to encourage and help others in the process, hope revives—and when people hope, they have something to start believing in again.

If we love what we do, we should never let setbacks derail our hopes and dreams. As Paul said in 1 Corinthians 13:13 NLT: "There are three things that will endure—faith, hope, and love." Never underestimate the power of any of these attributes in affecting your life.

Remember, Godly hope will never disappoint.

TODAY I WILL...

☑ be happy with what I already have

☑ reject the feeling that I need to "keep up with the Joneses"

☑ acknowledge that having Jesus in my life is more than enough

GODLINESS WITH CONTENTMENT
IS GREAT GAIN.

1 TIMOTHY 6:6 KJV

What is your motivation for excelling in your work? Do you feel driven to succeed so that you can afford that bigger car, house, or television set? Are you hoping that your next promotion and raise will finally allow you to catch up with your bills and start to pull ahead?

It is interesting to note that Jesus never told us we had a choice between serving God and the devil, but rather that we could serve either God or worldly wealth—in other words, money. Do you find yourself worrying more about paying your credit card bill than praising God for His blessings in your life? Do you find that you are more motivated to get that next raise than to please God? If so, perhaps you need to reconsider for a moment who is really your master.

Those who are truly successful financially have learned one thing: The only way to keep money from mastering you is to master it. They don't let money force them to work longer than they need to or keep them away from their families; they have learned to be content with what they have now, while also working industriously in the time they are on the job. They use their money to build stability for the future rather than buy luxuries for today that will put them into debt. They look at their families, their peace of mind, and the joy of not owing anyone else and call it a blessing from God.

Is it time for you to get out of the rat race? The first step is to learn to be content with what you already have and avoid getting sucked into the game of always needing more.

Remember, riches are
far more than just money.

TODAY I WILL...

☑ try to recognize and appreciate all that God has done for me

☑ plug into His plan and purpose for my life

☑ make an investment in my future—my eternal future

"THIS IS HOW MUCH GOD LOVED THE WORLD: HE GAVE HIS SON, HIS ONE AND ONLY SON. AND THIS IS WHY: SO THAT NO ONE NEED BE DESTROYED; BY BELIEVING IN HIM, ANYONE CAN HAVE A WHOLE AND LASTING LIFE."

JOHN 3:16 MSG

When God created you, He was making an investment. He sent you into the world expecting a return. He gave you a measure of the same thing He gave to everyone else—from the richest to the poorest—the same 24 hours a day, 168 hours a week, 52 weeks a year. He gave each of us unique talents to make our way in the world, and over time He blessed us with certain treasures that we could use to reinvest in our families and others. He sent us into the world hoping and planning for our success, but also knowing we could fail abysmally. Certainly there was a risk involved in doing this; but in the world of investments, the greater the risk, the greater the potential return.

However, God is not a fool. He hedged His investment in us by sending His Son to redeem us from failure if we should fall. He laid out a plan and purpose for our lives; then He provided wisdom, knowledge, and spiritual blessings for us to use to accomplish those plans. He has provided us with all we need pertaining to life and godliness. He then leaves His provision for us to either plug into or let it sit by the wayside while we try to struggle through on our own.

If we are truly trusting God and living with Him as our Lord, then fulfilling His divine plans and dreams for us should be our top priority; for only in Him will we ever be all that we can be. Take the time today to go to God and see how He wants you to handle that next project or spend that extra day off. The truth is that He already knows the best way for you to proceed—simply listen for His instructions.

Remember, God will never walk out on His investment in you.

TODAY I WILL...

☑ realize I already have enough to be happy right now

☑ not let that satisfaction keep me from helping others

☑ sow to my future and reap only from my past

"YOU'RE BLESSED WHEN YOU'RE CONTENT
WITH JUST WHO YOU ARE—NO MORE, NO LESS.
THAT'S THE MOMENT YOU FIND YOURSELVES PROUD
OWNERS OF EVERYTHING THAT CAN'T BE BOUGHT."

MATTHEW 5:5 MSG

Too often people mistake contentment with complacency. Contentment is the ability to look at what you have and say, "This is enough to make me happy." Complacency is when that contentment turns to self-satisfaction, thinking that you have enough in yourself to be happy. Contentment looks to God for satisfaction and sufficiency regardless of material possessions; complacency looks to material possessions and says, "Ah, I have done so well. Now I can sit back and be satisfied with myself."

Jesus illustrated the difference between the two in a parable He told of the rich man and his barns. When he saw that his barns were filled to the brim, his first thought was to build bigger ones to hold his extra to keep it for himself. His second thought was that now he could sit back and do no more work; eating, drinking, and spending what he had on himself. Yet the next day he would die and not be able to take any of it with him. He would leave nothing on earth but a legacy of amassing wealth to himself. As Jesus then said, "So is the man who stores up treasure for himself, and is not rich toward God" (Luke 12:21 NASB).

Being content with what we have is a key not only to living a happy, full life, but also to building the financial stability that will give our family and loved ones the education and care we want them to have. Complacency is to turn that contentment inward and take care only of ourselves. Since it is only what we do for others that will outlast us, we need to invest long-term before we give in to short-term impulses to please only ourselves.

Remember, "Where your treasure is, there your heart will be also."

(Matthew 6:21 NIV)

Today I Will...

- ☑ throw away my past grudges
- ☑ walk in constant forgiveness rather than feeling slighted by others
- ☑ not let myself get bogged down with what others say or do

Love . . . keeps no record of when
it has been wronged.

1 Corinthians 13:5 nlt

God doesn't suggest that we forgive others for their sakes as much as He wants us to forgive others for our own sake. The bitterness that comes from unforgiveness hampers us, not those that we have a grudge against. The subtlety of that bitterness is like the constant eating away at the base of a dam—once the base is weakened enough, the whole thing will come down.

Bitterness colors our world, darkens our outlook, and hampers us from reaching out in love. It sends a message to our hearts that if we reach out, we will only be hurt again. Bitterness is like carbon monoxide to our dreams; it will suffocate them if it is not replaced with the pure oxygen of love.

Unforgiveness is a burden not worth carrying. We need to realize that we must release it quickly in order to prevent damage to our aspirations and dreams. No matter how well-founded it is, it will never do anything but bring us down—and that is the last thing we need if we want to walk in all the good things God has for us.

*Remember, unforgiveness
only hurts you.*

TODAY I WILL...

☑ be willing to believe the best for my future

☑ trust God more than chance or my own abilities

☑ dream about my future and that of my loved ones

WRITE THE VISION, AND MAKE IT PLAIN.

HABAKKUK 2:2 KJV

According to pastor, author, and motivational speaker Myles Munroe, planning is a means of exercising your faith for what you believe God is leading you to do with your future. By writing your plan down and making it plain on paper, you are setting before you something to believe in—that your future can be as great as your hopes and dreams.

Many of us are afraid to write such things down because we want to be flexible. But what is really hindering us is fear—fear that we could hope for something too great to come about or fear that our dreams won't come true. We seem to unconsciously assume that by not having specific hopes or dreams for our future, we can't be disappointed. However, too often people who think this way are nothing but disappointed. They feel there is something they've missed in their lives because they never accomplished anything worthwhile.

Take time today to do some planning. When you look in your heart, what is it that you would really like to accomplish? When would you like your work to reflect the dream God has put in your heart? What do you want for your loved ones in the next five to twenty-five to fifty years? How about for your church and community? If you are ever going to make your dreams real, perhaps it is time to start now by committing these details to paper rather than just leaving them to chance.

Remember, people very often get what they hope for. What are you hoping for?

TODAY I WILL...

☑ dream beyond my limitations

☑ depend on the Creator of all
things for answers

☑ rest in His power rather than
my own

I WISDOM DWELL WITH PRUDENCE, AND FIND OUT
KNOWLEDGE OF WITTY INVENTIONS.

PROVERBS 8:12 KJV

You may have heard it said that "Necessity is the mother of invention," but this adage is not necessarily true. In fact, necessity only lays the seed in the right place for an idea to grow. And where does that seed grow? In the fertile imagination of the inventor. Thus, if anything, necessity is the father of invention—and imagination is its mother.

Are you facing a problem today that seems insurmountable? So did Thomas Edison in inventing the light bulb; how else would you describe his over two thousand failures? However, in the end, his ingenuity and persistence paid off. Yours will, too, if you stick to it.

God longs to give you the answers you need to the problems you face. Your imagination can be the canvas of Christ if you will let it—a place where He will paint the answers to your problems if you will only turn to Him. Never forget that the One who created the mountains and the stars is within you. He measured the seas with a drop of water in His hand. No difficulty is too big for Him to solve.

Remember, Jesus is the answer.

TODAY I WILL...

☑ be prompt in returning favors or things I have borrowed

☑ honor those who have authority over me

☑ repay my debts promptly

OWE NO ONE ANYTHING
EXCEPT TO LOVE ONE ANOTHER.

ROMANS 13:8 NKJV

When Paul spoke of submitting to and honoring authority in Romans 13, it is interesting that he closed the discussion with this thought: "Owe no one anything except to love them." In other words, as far as tariffs and taxes were concerned, pay them promptly and fully according to the law. We are to speak respectfully and honor those who represent the government, whether we are talking about the President's last address on television or the police officer who pulls us over because we missed a stop sign. Many have preached by extension that this scripture also means paying our bills and invoices in a timely manner, returning things that we have borrowed as promptly as we can, and running our businesses in such a way that we "owe no one anything except to love them."

The implication of this interpretation is worth considering, in that the only debt we will never be able to pay off is that of "love." How can we, for instance, "owe love" to someone who clearly has never loved us? Why should we be nice to those who are cruel to us or respect authority that is immoral, corrupt, or just plain disagreeable? How do we "owe" anything to such people?

We are to repay the debt of love not because we owe them anything, but because we owe everything to Jesus for what His love did for us in providing us forgiveness, redemption, and salvation. It is truly a debt we can never repay. Because Jesus doesn't need these things from us, He requires that we pay them to those who do. The debt of love is one we need to remember to make payments on daily for the rest of our lives.

Remember, we forgive graciously
because we have been
so graciously forgiven.

Today I Will...

- ☑ be quick to hear and obey God's voice
- ☑ keep things simple
- ☑ focus on service rather than striving for advancement

"Happy are those whose greatest
desire is to do what God requires;
God will satisfy them fully!"

Matthew 5:6 tev

In a busy square in Capernaum, the disciples finally worked up the nerve to ask Jesus a question that had been bothering them for some time: "Who is the greatest in the kingdom of heaven?"

In response, Jesus turned to a child running by. The child may have been on an important errand for her parents, or it could have been a boy in the midst of a game of tag running from a friend. Likely the child was occupied in something else, but at Jesus' call, the child stopped whatever he or she was doing and came over and stood before Jesus. Then Jesus answered the disciples: "Assuredly, I say to you, unless you are converted and become as little children, you will by no means enter the kingdom of heaven. Therefore whoever humbles himself *as this little child* is the greatest in the kingdom of heaven" (Matthew 18:3-4 NKJV, emphasis added).

Though Jesus commended a childlike nature as a condition for being in God's kingdom, He noted something particular about this one child that made him or her stand out. What was it? It was that the child obeyed immediately, dropped whatever game or errand, and came to stand before Jesus, ready for whatever He might request next.

Is such obedience possible in the busy world of today? Regardless of the importance of what we are doing, or how involved we are in it, we had better make sure that we are ready to be just that quick to obey if Jesus calls on us.

Remember, to obey when Jesus calls is better than trying to make up for it with sacrifices later. (See 1 Samuel 15:22.)

Today I Will...

- ☑ take every opportunity to see things from other people's perspectives

- ☑ be ready to show mercy for true repentance

- ☑ be ready to show true repentance that I might receive mercy

"Blessed are the merciful,
for they will be shown mercy."

Matthew 5:7 niv

In the competitive environment of business, the value of a second chance is difficult to estimate on a spreadsheet, calculate in a profit and loss statement, or record on a performance evaluation. There are times when all of the evidence points to letting someone go—yet at the same time, it is exactly the wrong thing to do. True mercy, however, is not just giving someone a second chance, but staying diligent in one's management of resources and staff so that layoffs or dismissals for performance reasons are dealt with before they become big enough to cost people their jobs.

One thing we should know from the Bible is that there will always be cycles of prosperity and lack on the earth, as in the seven years of abundance and then seven years of famine from which God helped Joseph deliver Egypt and Israel. As Ecclesiastes 3:1,6 NKJV says: "To everything there is a season, a time for every purpose under heaven: . . . a time to gain, and a time to lose; a time to keep, and a time to throw away." We cannot believe that times of increase and profit will last forever. If companies spent all of their money during the time when things are going well, what can we expect when things slow down?

The wise and merciful businessperson will be prepared for such occurrences, putting money aside for bad times so that when things slow down for a time, the company will not need to lay off employees just to keep the doors open. Planning for such eventualities and using wisdom in managing resources can give employees that second chance to make it work without even threatening their personal futures. After all, true riches are measured by the lives that we touch for the better, not what we can store up in barns or banks on the earth.

Remember, the hand of the diligent enriches all around it. (See Proverbs 10:4.)

Today I Will...

☑ purpose to seek God in the midst of urgent demands

☑ accept that there is no season of my life that I can do without God

☑ let God create an inner peace in me that will shine to the outside world

"You're blessed when you get your inside world—your mind and heart—put right. Then you can see God in the outside world."

Matthew 5:8 MSG

What is the really important thing in life? It always seems that if we can just get the answer to this question, then everything else will work out around us. But the answer seems to change depending on the place we are in our lives, the time of month it is and what bills are due, the season of the year it is and what activities each brings, as well as any number of factors that can change our focus in a given moment. It seems that wherever we are in our lives, we believe that just as soon as we get through this next thing—this next project is done, soccer season is over, the play is finally performed, that next promotion comes, or whatever else we have going on—we can finally relax a bit and get a better direction for our lives.

Yet hearing from God hasn't changed in six thousand years. It is still done the same way today as it was by Adam, Abraham, Joseph, and Moses. Perhaps none of them had so many other "noises" around them to constantly contend with. But even in the relatively quiet and slower-paced world they lived in, only those who truly sought God heard Him. To hear God's voice, they had to go out of their way to find a quiet place, sit, pray, and listen patiently for the answer. And God didn't reveal himself to them all at once. Over time they got to know Him more and more as they showed the desire to know Him more and more—whether they were in a field tending sheep or in the midst of a battle to protect God's people.

We need to learn to do the same. We need to seek God every day regardless of our circumstances. Once we get that right, we might start seeing more of Him in the world around us.

Remember, God is still God, regardless of what is happening around us.

Today I Will...

- ☑ choose my words wisely to build others up and encourage them
- ☑ speak hope and optimism
- ☑ listen to what I say and try to keep my words in line with what I hope to accomplish

Let your conversation be gracious and effective so that you will have the right answer for everyone.

Colossians 4:6 nlt

In his epistle to the Church, James likens the tongue—quite literally the words we speak—to two things: a bit in a horse's mouth and the rudder of a great ship. (See James 3:3-6.) His meaning is quite clear: The words we speak steer or direct our lives more definitely than any external circumstances. Though great winds can drive a ship, it is the till that sets the course; and though a horse is much stronger than a person, a tiny pull in one direction or the other on the reins is enough to make the great animal change course.

So, too, is wisdom often measured in words—or sometimes the lack of them. Proverbs 17:28 NKJV tells us, "Even a fool is counted wise when he holds his peace; when he shuts his lips, he is considered perceptive." Thus what we say, and when we say it, can be very important; and, more often than not, leaving things unsaid may be the wisest course of all.

As you go about your day today, listen to what comes out of your mouth. Are you speaking encouraging and uplifting words to others that are seasoned with the salt of God's love and truth? Or are the words you speak more to lift yourself up in the eyes of others and appease your ego? Perhaps your conversation is neither of these, but only frivolous chattering.

If the words we speak are capable of directing us towards our future goals—or more importantly, directing others towards Jesus—isn't it time we take a solid account of what we say and do to determine whether it is profitable or not?

Remember, we generally speak about what is most abundant in our hearts.

TODAY I WILL...

☑ be a peacemaker

☑ not let my anger lead to strife

☑ be firm in my dedication to true "win-win" negotiations in all matters

"GOD BLESSES THOSE WHO WORK FOR PEACE, FOR THEY WILL BE CALLED THE CHILDREN OF GOD."

MATTHEW 5:9 NLT

In the hectic, high-pressure, and highly competitive world of business, it is often difficult to find peace for ourselves, let alone to help others find it. Yet if we are looking to be representatives of God's kingdom on the earth— "Christ's ambassadors of reconciliation" as Paul infers we are in 2 Corinthians 5—then building peace and improving relationships between individuals and companies, even if they are competitors, is part of our calling.

Is it possible to be in conflict without strife, or as it has been said so many times before, "to disagree without being disagreeable"? What was Jesus' example in such things? When He called the Pharisees and Sadducees "a brood of vipers" (Matthew 12:34), was He just trying to stir up trouble, or did He intend to awaken them to their plight of being far from what God had called them to be?

The latter must obviously have been the case—and if so, our methods should be driven by the same motives. If we are at times harsh or uncompromising, it should be with the point of bringing reconciliation, not strife and division. In some ways, we have a much more difficult part to play in such interactions than Jesus did; He could know He was not being self-righteous in His words. We have more difficulty making such judgments. So, if anything, we should err on the side of grace and love.

In your dealings today, look for opportunities to be a minister of reconciliation, led by peace and worthy of your high calling in Christ.

Remember, it is the goodness of God that leads to repentance.

(See Romans 2:4.)

TODAY I WILL...

☑ remember the good things God has done for me

☑ be encouraged by the testimonies of God's goodness in the lives of others

☑ find the reason for hope in any situation

I WOULD HAVE DESPAIRED UNLESS I HAD BELIEVED
THAT I WOULD SEE THE GOODNESS OF THE LORD
IN THE LAND OF THE LIVING.

PSALM 27:13 NASB

In today's world where the media bombards us with constant negative news, imagery, and dialogue, it is far too easy to forget the good things that God is doing in our world. Despair, hopelessness, and general negativity are constant threats to our daily outlook. The pessimists seem to get it right much more than do the optimists. How can we impact a world so full of problems that our greatest efforts to do good seem easily overcome?

We have to remember the power of light over darkness—that even a small candle can light a dark room enough for us to see our next step clearly. While many would gladly sit on the sideline and criticize, only those who dare to hope accomplish much that is worthwhile. While the odds against success are intense, new ventures still start up and succeed regularly. Can we truly afford to let pessimism keep us from following our dreams?

We have to take Jesus' advice in the matter. Like the person planning to build a tower, counting the costs first and ensuring that everything needed to succeed has been procured, we must put in the hard work necessary to build towards our own success. Don't let pessimism sap from you your energy and determination. Believe you will see the goodness of God, and then be diligent to follow the dreams He has given you. Let the critics and pessimists say whatever they like. Learn from them, but don't let them take away your hope and faith in what you are doing.

Remember, God's plans are for your ultimate good, even if they take you through some dry and barren places.

TODAY I WILL...

☑ seek God's wisdom and lean on His grace

☑ pursue His will with all of my heart

☑ extend God's love to those who are no worse than I would be without it

"YOU'RE BLESSED WHEN YOU'RE AT THE END OF YOUR ROPE. WITH LESS OF YOU THERE IS MORE OF GOD AND HIS RULE."

MATTHEW 5:3 MSG

Can we reconcile humility and confidence? Can we be both meek and ambitious at the same time? Is it possible to aggressively push our companies or enterprises forward while at the same time recognizing we are poor in spirit and greatly in need of our Savior's reminder that without Him we are lost?

The Bible tells us that Moses was the meekest man who ever walked the earth (Numbers 12:3 KJV), yet it was Moses who stood before almighty God and told Him He was wrong in threatening to violate His "contract" with the people of Israel. Imagine this confrontation for a moment. Not long before, God had offered the people of Israel the chance to know Him and come before Him on their own without Moses as mediator, but when they stood at the foot of the mountain before Him, they could say nothing but, "Moses, you go. We'll stay here. Just tell us whatever it is He tells you, and we'll do it." (See Deuteronomy 5:23-27.) Before that same awe-inspiring God, the meekest man on earth stood and pleaded for what was right.

Humility and meekness are not cowardice, but rather the ability to stand with conviction before God and say, "Lord, I am nothing without You"—an act which is perhaps the most ambitious and courageous we can ever aspire to. It is an act of true faith in God. There is never a more purpose-driven, confident, and ambitious person than the one who knows his or her place is fully depending and trusting in the Lord.

Remember, when we are weak,
then He is strong on our behalf.

TODAY I WILL...

☑ invest in eternity

☑ manage my money better

☑ sow to the future more than spend for today

"SO IF YOU HAVE NOT BEEN TRUSTWORTHY IN
HANDLING WORLDLY WEALTH,
WHO WILL TRUST YOU WITH TRUE RICHES?"

LUKE 16:11 NIV

Any investment program that does not look to the future is worthless. Why invest in something that will not be around tomorrow? Edwin Louis Cole used to say, "We sow to the future and reap from the past." If this is true, then the most valuable things to invest in are those that will be around the longest. Those of us who plan to spend our ultimate retirement in Heaven should think more about investing in eternity than in anything else.

It has been said that "you can't take it with you," but that is not entirely true. What we invest in that has eternal worth will go with us, namely the people that are touched through how we invest our time, talents, and treasures. Luke 16:9 NIV tells us to "use worldly wealth to gain friends for yourselves, so that when it is gone, you will be welcomed into eternal dwellings."

Any investment program we plug into will demand wisdom and diligence if it is to be successful. We need to remember that not only should our plans include providing for our children's college education, a new home or car, our retirement, or any of a number of other worthy goals, but also investing in that which is eternal, whether it be a coworker, the needy who come to our churches, or the poor in a faraway land. Ten thousand years from now, which will have been the wisest investments? Only those that we can "take with us!"

Remember, what you have in this world is only temporary.

Today I Will...

- ☑ treat the place I work as if it were my own business

- ☑ be a good steward of the time I have promised to others

- ☑ be frugal with the resources of others and treat them as I would my own

If you cannot be trusted with what belongs to someone else, who will give you something that will be your own?

Luke 16:12 CEV

Paper clips, pens, photocopies, Internet access, long-distance phone calls, time around the water cooler, and a myriad of other "small" things are often a temptation for small acts of theft from our employers. They may just be little things that our supervisors may not even seem to care about, but habits of unfaithfulness in little things too often grow into larger and larger violations of privilege until we have set down a pattern of unfaithfulness and slothfulness in all of our work habits. The Message Bible says it this way: "If you're honest in small things, you'll be honest in big things; If you're a crook in small things, you'll be a crook in big things. If you're not honest in small jobs, who will put you in charge of the store?" (Luke 16:10-12 MSG).

Employees often feel unappreciated in their work and somehow subconsciously justify these little acts as entitlements they have because they are not making the money they feel they should, are not being treated with the respect they feel they deserve, or have been passed up for some advancement, project, or opportunity they feel they have earned. But the fact of the matter is that even little acts of theft are still theft. The employee who swipes office pens or spends time browsing the Internet for personal reasons on company time is no better than the little kid who shoplifts candy from the local grocery store. We think we get away with it if we are not caught, but all we do is solidify a pattern of unfaithfulness and cutting corners to get ahead rather than solidifying the work habits that will be a blessing to our lives.

Remember, how faithful you are in the little things you have today will determine how much you are trusted with tomorrow.

TODAY I WILL...

☑ take an account of whether I control my money or my money controls me

☑ do good with what falls within my influence

☑ dedicate my resources to build my Lord's kingdom as well as secure my family's future

---

"NO SERVANT CAN SERVE TWO MASTERS. FOR EITHER HE WILL HATE ONE AND LOVE THE OTHER, OR BE LOYAL TO ONE AND DESPISE THE OTHER. YOU CANNOT SERVE GOD AND RICHES!"

LUKE 6:13 ISV

In his book *The Purpose-Driven Life*, Pastor Rick Warren says, "Money is both a test and a trust. God uses finances to teach us to trust Him. . . . God watches how we use money to test how trustworthy we are."[1] When money goes from a test and trust to lord of our lives, determining how and where we spend our time, then something is seriously out of place. If we are ever going to get to a place where money doesn't control our lives and dictate our actions, then we are going to have to get to a place were we control money and dictate what it will do.

The fact is that money is a force in our world that makes things happen, and those things are generally very negative unless good people determine what it does. Many people believe that we are stewards of what God has given us, but then they look only to what is in their immediate influence as the responsibility of that stewardship. The Bible tells us that we are stewards of all that is on the earth. Is it really responsible stewardship to allow the corrupt and selfish to control most of the earth's resources?

How we work in our businesses and manage the wealth of our companies as well as how we manage our personal finances determines the faithfulness of our stewardship. We need to be mindful each day about how we will answer when we are called to give account before Jesus on that final day. Will you be among the good and faithful stewards God has left to be responsible for His resources on the earth?

Remember, the only way to avoid money mastering us is to master it.

TODAY I WILL...

☑ carry God's principles and ways in the forefront of my mind and my heart

☑ look for God's way in the midst of the confusion of the world's ways

☑ live as a beacon of God's light in the midst of a selfish and money-oriented workplace

IF ALL YOU WANT IS YOUR OWN WAY, FLIRTING WITH THE WORLD EVERY CHANCE YOU GET, YOU END UP ENEMIES OF GOD AND HIS WAY. AND DO YOU SUPPOSE GOD DOESN'T CARE?

JAMES 4:4-5 MSG

There may be no greater deception in the world of business than a sense of entitlement. While entry-level employees may be deceived by it to the point of justifying the theft of pens or copy paper, upper-level managers can fall to using it to manipulate those they supervise—or abuse their company credit cards to buy personal items or expensive lunches. CEOs and presidents also fall into its grasp to justify huge raises and bonuses for themselves, while there are large layoffs or cutbacks in their companies. Entitlement allows them to disregard the truth and ethical principles in order to satisfy selfish desires.

James tells us that we deceive ourselves when we hear what is right, but don't do it. (See James 1:22.) This deception occurs in business when facts and figures are presented to the decision-makers, but instead of securing the future of their companies and employees, they choose instead to secure their own positions or financial situations. People aren't hypocrites because they have consciously chosen to be so, but because they have allowed themselves to be deceived. Then, walking in that deception, they spin the facts to justify their actions to others, spreading their deception to those who trust them.

Take a moment today and look for areas in which you may be deceiving yourself about what you are doing at work. Pray that God will reveal these areas to you and bring people into your life who can help you see the truth clearly. Only by clearing your vision can you see your way ahead to do the right things and accomplish your goals.

Remember, where there is no clear vision, there is no self-control.

TODAY I WILL...

- ☑ take time to reevaluate my goals

- ☑ eliminate distractions from my life that eat up time that should be used to accomplish something

- ☑ let the past be the past and focus on what is ahead

I AM FOCUSING ALL MY ENERGIES ON THIS ONE THING: FORGETTING THE PAST AND LOOKING FORWARD TO WHAT LIES AHEAD, I STRAIN TO REACH THE END OF THE RACE AND RECEIVE THE PRIZE FOR WHICH GOD, THROUGH CHRIST JESUS, IS CALLING US UP TO HEAVEN.

PHILIPPIANS 3:13-14 NLT

Motivational speaker and minister Bob Harrison has often said, "Setting goals can be one of the most dangerous things anyone ever does." Why is that? Because we often remember to set goals in business and finances but forget to set goals in more personal areas such as family, spiritual growth, health, and service to others.

Goals have a way of bringing focus in our lives to certain matters, and thus pull attention away from other areas of our lives deemed less important by omission. By having goals in only one or two areas of our lives, we inadvertently determine to fail in all others. Goals create focus and determine how we will allocate our resources, time, talent, and treasure.

When we set goals, we need to determine to look at all the areas of our lives and give them equal attention so that our focus is on what is truly important and not just on what will get us the greatest advancement in our careers or the most financial success. Just as Paul used the power of his focus to push ahead to accomplish what God called him to do, so should we—whether that be in business, our church involvement, building our family's futures, maintaining our health, or building the character within ourselves to be able to handle greater responsibility tomorrow than we have today.

Remember, what you focus on will define who you are. Are you focused on the right things?

TODAY I WILL...

☑ not give in to the temptation to be a workaholic

☑ balance the value of what I do at work with what I do at home, at church, and in my community

☑ analyze my goals from the perspective of eternity

A VERY LITTLE FOOD EATEN IN PEACE IS BETTER
THAN TWICE AS MUCH EARNED FROM OVERWORK
AND CHASING THE WIND.

ECCLESIASTES 4:6 CEV

What are the basics a person needs for living? Food, shelter, and clothing? A reasonable means of transportation and fulfilling work that provides enough for the basic needs of one's family? Just how much do we really need to survive in this world? How much is enough?

If we live in a developed country, we fool ourselves if we say that God meets only our needs and not our wants. The fact of the matter is we have several times more than enough to meet the basic needs of life, yet what do we do with the extra? The question is really not, "How much is enough?" but "How much more than enough is enough?" And since we have more than enough, what is our responsibility regarding the abundance that we have?

Paul said of those as privileged as we are, "Command those who are rich in this present age not to be haughty, nor to trust in uncertain riches but in the living God, who gives us richly all things to enjoy. Let them do good, that they be rich in good works, ready to give, willing to share, storing up for themselves a good foundation for the time to come, that they may lay hold on eternal life" (1 Timothy 6:17-19).

What are you doing now with your wealth—your time, talent, and treasure—that is having an impact on eternity? How about the eternal destiny of your family and loved ones? What will another late night at the office accomplish that will truly last?

Remember, we should not define ourselves by what we have, but by the lives we touch.

TODAY I WILL...

☑ work as if God were my supervisor and not other people

☑ consider my motives for what I do each day

☑ scrutinize my attitudes towards those I serve either at work or as a volunteer

THEN I OBSERVED ALL THE WORK AND AMBITION MOTIVATED BY ENVY. WHAT A WASTE! SMOKE. AND SPITTING INTO THE WIND.

ECCLESIASTES 4:4 MSG

What motivates you in your work? The desire to be the head of the company? Keeping up with what the neighbors have? Trying to outperform your colleagues to get the next available advancement? If so, Solomon is speaking to you. If you are motivated by envy, jealousy, or competition to get ahead, what you are doing is merely smoke and spitting in the wind. What a waste. Why? Because even if you get what you are after, your selfish motivation will undermine your reward.

The Bible has great advice about serving those who have rule over us: "Obey them not only to win their favor when their eye is on you, but like slaves of Christ, doing the will of God from your heart. Serve wholeheartedly, as if you were serving the Lord, not men" (Ephesians 6:6-7 NIV). In other words, don't just work for your employer to accomplish the tasks for the day, but work for what will last into eternity—the fruit of the Spirit (Galatians 5:22) you develop as you go about the duties of each.

Is it possible to get to know your Lord and Savior better as you attend to the affairs of this world? It depends largely on your motivation and how you approach the challenges you face each day. Challenges can either exercise your righteousness or undermine it; the choice is really up to you.

Remember, we will all face tests, trials, and temptations in this world; whether they bring us closer to God or not is determined by the attitude with which we face them.

Today I Will . . .

☑ find a fresh start towards my goals and dreams

☑ lay aside, but not repeat, the mistakes of the past

☑ focus on Jesus' example of how to win the race I am in

Strip down, start running—and never quit! No extra spiritual fat, no parasitic sins. Keep your eyes on Jesus, who both began and finished this race we're in. Study how he did it. Because he never lost sight of where he was headed—that exhilarating finish in and with God—he could put up with anything along the way: cross, shame, whatever.

Hebrews 12:1-2 msg

What a gift a new day can be. Regardless of the past, the sun always rises on a new day, even if clouds veil it. And with it comes the promise of starting anew the race set before us. Each new day presents us with the opportunity to set aside whatever happened the day before and again put one foot in front of the other towards our goals and dreams. Yet often before we have the strength to press ahead, we must look behind us and ask forgiveness for the mistakes and excesses of the days before so that we have nothing hindering us as we move forward.

Psalm 103:12 NIV tells us: "As far as the east is from the west, so far has he removed our transgressions from us." In other words, when God forgives us of past mistakes, He also forgets them. As Corrie ten Boom once said, such sins are "now cast into the deepest sea and a sign is put up that says, 'NO FISHING ALLOWED.'" What is past is past with Him. If we choose to fish our sins out again and let them hinder us, that is our doing, not His.

Obviously for the writer of this passage in Hebrews, the key to accomplishing whatever is before us, no matter how intense or unpleasant it may be, is to learn to put past mistakes behind and not let them trip us up again as we move forward. Of course, doing so also means not letting those same mistakes trip us up again in the future. Thus we can move forward towards what He has set before us, unhindered and unburdened. Only in His forgiveness is the true freedom to succeed.

Remember, He is faithful and just to forgive us. (See 1 John 1:9.)

TODAY I WILL...

- ☑ listen
- ☑ take time to hear what is on the hearts of others
- ☑ discern God's voice speaking to me

HOW BOLD AND FREE WE THEN BECOME IN HIS
PRESENCE, FREELY ASKING ACCORDING TO HIS
WILL, SURE THAT HE'S LISTENING.

1 JOHN 5:14 MSG

Taking time to genuinely listen might be the greatest good or the kindest compliment we have to give. Fully listening and truly hearing the heart of another is nearly a lost art in modern society. Author David Michael Levin has written, "The very limited development of our capacity for listening is responsible for much suffering and misery in life."[2] If we are to demonstrate God's healing mercy and grace in this earth, we must learn to listen. God's most profound promise to us, after all, is that He hears.

Being fully present for others, fully engaged in their concerns, requires that we learn to be attentive. Unless we strive to hear the deepest cries, joys, desires, or aches within the hearts of others, we won't have the right words of encouragement, hope, or exhortation to offer. Carl Rogers once said, "A man's inability to communicate is a result of his failure to listen effectively, skillfully, and with understanding to another person."

Practice the art of listening today. Be the sounding board others are seeking, a source of reassurance because you truly hear. Effective listening requires compassion and empathy. Well-known author Jane Austen once said, "There is no charm equal to tenderness of heart." Practice the tender mercies spoken of in Proverbs by being a life-giving listener.

Remember, there may be no greater gift than the ability to listen.

TODAY I WILL...

- ☑ live the truth I know
- ☑ endeavor to authentically be what I desire to appear
- ☑ become the change I wish to see in the world

AS THE HUMAN BODY APART FROM THE SPIRIT IS
LIFELESS, SO FAITH APART FROM [ITS] WORKS OF
OBEDIENCE IS ALSO DEAD.

JAMES 2:26 AMP

So many of us mentally ascend to the truths we read in the Bible or hear preached on Sunday morning. We shout out "Amen!" and "Hallelujah!" and nod approvingly. We agree with the wisdom found in Proverbs, the promises found in Psalms, and the principles found throughout the Epistles. We preach the peace of the Gospel, the prosperity of the believer, and the provision of God the Father. Yet, in our daily lives, involving the moment-by-moment battles for our thoughts and minds, we often find we are losing ground—quickly sinking—suddenly overcome with anxiety, disappointment, and even despair.

This failure to trust God in our daily lives must grievously displease Him as it so loudly proclaims our self-centeredness. While others around us are in need, we are so absorbed in our own problems that we are unable to show mercy—or simply unavailable to do a good deed. If we desire to be blessed, we must be a blessing. If we hunger for peace, we must be peaceable. If we are in need of mercy, we must be merciful.

The enemy strives to take our eyes off God's goodness and grace and keep us focused on the world's lack and depravity. If we are to inspire hope, we must be expectant. If we are to see deliverance, we must show our exuberance for having been delivered. It is for good reason we are instructed in Philippians 4:4-8 to fill our minds with thoughts that are affirming, praiseworthy, and lovely.

Remember, it is with joy
we draw water from the wells
of salvation. (See Isaiah 12:3.)

TODAY I WILL...

☑ enjoy doing a good job

☑ be a blessing to my company

☑ let my effort and quality of performance speak for themselves

OBSERVE PEOPLE WHO ARE GOOD AT THEIR WORK—SKILLED WORKERS ARE ALWAYS IN DEMAND AND ADMIRED; THEY DON'T TAKE A BACK SEAT TO ANYONE.

PROVERBS 22:29 MSG

Office politics, nepotism, discrimination, favoritism—any of us who have been passed up for promotion have probably heard or even used one of these terms as an excuse to describe why the promotion didn't come our way. Yet should we be complaining? The Bible tells us that all authority—even unfair authority—is appointed by the Lord. (See Romans 13:1-2; 1 Peter 2:18-24.) When we don't get the rewards we believe we deserve, we should see it as an opportunity rather than a strike against us. Will we choose to trust in the Lord for our promotion or in our own strengths, skills, and abilities to "work the system"?

When Joseph was in his teens, he had a dream that he would one day be top dog in the nation of Israel (which at the time was just his family). However, what awaited him? Slavery, where he preformed incredibly well serving another and building his household, and imprisonment, his reward for his faithfulness to his master and God in rejecting the advances of Potiphar's wife. (See Genesis 37:36; 39:20.) For thirteen years, he suffered as the servant of others, each time, however, rising to a place of honor because of the sincerity of his obedience. Did he get bitter and curse his luck and the unfairness of his setbacks? We have no indication that he did so. Instead, we see that he obeyed his earthly masters "with fear and trembling, in singleness of heart, as unto Christ . . . doing the will of God from the heart" (Ephesians 6:5-6 KJV). For this obedience, he went from prison to vice-president in one day—all because he was faithful and sought God more than his own promotion.

Remember, God who sees what others don't is the true source of all promotion.

Today I Will...

☑ recognize that the work I do is not mundane if I do it as unto the Lord

☑ seek God's guidance in determining my priorities

☑ glorify God

TAKE YOUR EVERYDAY, ORDINARY LIFE—YOUR
SLEEPING, EATING, GOING-TO-WORK, AND
WALKING-AROUND LIFE—AND PLACE IT BEFORE
GOD AS AN OFFERING.

ROMANS 12:1 MSG

It is interesting what happens when we come to regard something as commonplace or ordinary. Whatever we do every day, though it may have been incredibly interesting and fascinating when we first started, can become boring with repetition, even though it may be incredibly interesting and fascinating to others. It may also happen that those we work with or for, though incredible people when we first met them, sink lower in our esteem as we become more familiar with them and realize that they are people subject to faults and mistakes just as the rest of us are. It becomes too easy to take for granted what we know well and get sloppy in our work or even become satisfied with just looking busy, whether we really accomplish anything or not.

Yet holding such activities before Jesus can change all of that. As with any true discipline, the nuances of what we do can become more fascinating through repetition and practice as we notice new aspects of what we do. With time and attention to detail comes expertise that allows us to do the same things more quickly and even better. The true success of any business or enterprise is often in the details others are too lazy to take care of or don't care enough to notice. Just as "the little foxes . . . spoil the vines" (Song of Solomon 2:15) so it is that little by little your business can grow and take a larger portion of the market. (See Exodus 23:30.)

Remember, since we have chosen the life of the Spirit, we must apply it to every detail of our lives. (See Galatians 5:25 MSG.)

TODAY I WILL...

- ☑ analyze my motives in all that I do
- ☑ stay true to what I say to others
- ☑ please Jesus

FIGURE OUT WHAT WILL PLEASE CHRIST,
AND THEN DO IT.

EPHESIANS 5:10 MSG

The word *integrity* has been thrown around in our modern business world to the point it is almost meaningless. In fact, it has become such a buzz word that the more people claim they have it, the less likely we are to think they really do. It has become such a part of the hype to try to "close the sale" that, in too many cases, it is losing its power to either positively influence our success or create the stability we need to found our businesses.

Yet true integrity has little to do with hype and everything to do with long-term dependability and faithfulness. Just as the integrity of steel is determined by the purity of its elements, which in turn determine its strength, so the integrity of our performance is determined by the purity of our motives and determines the reliability others can have in what we say. Personal integrity should be a characteristic we strive to live rather than using it to describe ourselves. Like many other attributes, if integrity is a quality we must point out to convince others we have it, then we probably don't have enough of it for others to notice on their own.

Yet living with integrity is truly not that difficult. We will do so naturally if we simply choose to live a life that would please Jesus. In order to do that, we must spend more time listening for His voice and less time trying to get Him to bless our plans. Take the time today to listen for what pleases Him the most—and then do it.

Remember, If you are willing and obedient, you shall eat the good of the land (Isaiah 1:19 NKJV).

TODAY I WILL...

☑ focus on my most important tasks first

☑ create blocks of time in my day that will not be interrupted by busywork

☑ organize my questions and requests so that they do not waste the time of others

DON'T WASTE YOUR TIME ON USELESS WORK,

MERE BUSYWORK.

EPHESIANS 5:11 MSG

One of the key points that time-management experts focus on to increase productivity is eliminating activities that waste time or do not promote progress towards goals. These activities can be different for each of us depending on what we do or what we need to accomplish in the next day, week, or month. (For example, while answering phone calls can be important for a salesperson, putting the phone on "do not disturb" or letting someone else take calls may be in order for someone who needs a block of time to focus on solving a problem, finishing a report, or creatively planning for the future.) There are times when staring out the window is appropriate to help us focus our thoughts or when getting enough rest is more important than working extra hours.

Look at the little time-stealers that eat up your workday. Eliminate or delegate these tasks in order to accomplish more. Perhaps working out of the office for a time could also increase your focus and help you accomplish more. The key is to find the balance and create the environment that will minimize or eliminate time-wasters from pulling at your attention so they do not compete with your ability to focus on your real work.

As Benjamin Franklin said, "Dost thou love life? Then do not squander time; for that's the stuff life is made of."

*Remember, time is
our most precious commodity
—spend it wisely.*

TODAY I WILL...

☑ not gossip and refuse to listen to it

☑ focus on the positive things in my company and industry

☑ speak only to encourage and build

WHERE THERE IS NO FUEL
A FIRE GOES OUT; WHERE THERE IS NO GOSSIP
ARGUMENTS COME TO AN END.

PROVERBS 26:20 CEV

It is not unusual that our workplaces are full of talk—and not all of that talk is worth the time it takes up. However, some conversations are worse than others, and often the gossip that is aimed at self-promotion and undermining others is the worst of all. Gossip creates the fuel for the fires of arguments, conflict, and strife that can smolder in an office to the point of destroying careers or even the company itself.

As Christians, however, we should know that it is not only the outward, overt effects of gossip that are dangerous, but also the inward spiritual ramifications that being involved in gossip can cause for us. Gossip, whether true or false, builds bitterness and self-righteousness in our hearts toward the person being discussed. We are building an invisible barrier of contempt, disrespect, and often jealousy between that person and ourselves. Over time, just as with unforgiveness, this barrier creeps into our attitudes and hardens our hearts towards all other people. The gossip ends up doing more harm to us than anyone else.

Though we know we should avoid gossip, it still has a tingling allure that makes us feel better about ourselves for the fleeting moments that we give in to it. Yet if we are to avoid its sting, we need to steer clear of gossip altogether. God gave us the ability to speak so we could communicate together to do great things. Don't let that gift turn into a curse. Control what you say and what you hear to keep your thoughts focused on what is pure, lovely, and of good report! (See Philippians 4:8.)

Remember, what you say directs your life. (See James 3:4-5.)

TODAY I WILL...

☑ inspire hope

☑ practice expectancy

☑ think thoughts of possibility

IN HOPE WE HAVE BEEN SAVED.

ROMANS 8:24 NASB

In today's bad-news-driven world, it can be all too easy to fall into the habit of expecting the worst or to become overwhelmed with negative thoughts, disappointments, and offenses. We are daily bombarded with reports of economic tension and social unrest. Increasing financial uncertainties and widespread political instability can shake our confidence and sense of personal security. Sometimes staying hopeful and optimistic about the future is truly a battle. As Kouzes and Posner, authors of *The Leadership Challenge*, write: "Without hope, there can be no courage—and this is not the time or place for the timid. . . . Leaders must summon their will if they are to. . .triumph against the odds."[3]

Hope is indeed the anchor of our souls (Hebrews 6:19), and the courage to be hopeful is thus the source of our stability and steady progress when we face rough seas and uncertain times. The Bible says that whosoever hopes in God will not be put to shame. (See Romans 5:5.) We are instructed that we should not lean on our own understanding but instead acknowledge and trust in God in all our ways. (See Proverbs 3:5-6.) There is no need to give in to anxiety and struggle. If we truly trust in God—fearing not, but believing in His promises for direction, protection, and provision—we can have hope at all times, in all things.

"Hope enables people to transcend the difficulties of today and envision the potentialities of tomorrow," say Kouzes and Posner. "Hope enables people to find the will and the way to unleash greatness."[4]

Remember, the faith and determination to achieve anything starts with hope.

TODAY I WILL...

☑ be wholehearted

☑ eliminate distractions (but not rest and recreation) from my goals and activities

☑ be single-minded and purpose-driven

MAKE ME TRULY HAPPY BY AGREEING
WHOLEHEARTEDLY WITH EACH OTHER, LOVING ONE
ANOTHER, AND WORKING TOGETHER WITH ONE
HEART AND PURPOSE.

PHILIPPIANS 2:2 NLT

Psalm 133 tells us that there is an incredible blessing on people who live together in unity. The Bible also implies that the same unity is key in our lives as individuals—in keeping our goals, motives, and pursuits adhering to one central guiding purpose in our lives. As James 1:8 KJV tells us "A double minded man is unstable in all his ways." In the same way, those who serve two masters are as ineffective as those who serve themselves above their employers or supervisors. They have divided loyalties that ultimately cause them to act in their own interest rather than that of the company or organization they manage. This disunity leads to undermining others in their pursuit to build their own kingdom rather than building the organizations they were hired to promote and develop.

The only true unity on earth, however, comes from serving God above all else. Setting this priority places everything else in proper order, and our performance is enhanced rather than divided. Walking in the fruits of the Spirit in true submission to God should also allow us to keep focused on what our employers are asking us to do—unless, of course, these expectations contradict Scripture, in which case we should be looking for employment elsewhere. As Galatians 5:16 KJV says, "Walk in the Spirit, and ye shall not fulfil the lust of the flesh." If we will follow God's leading in our hearts, we can set selfishness aside to accomplish our true goals and purposes.

It is only when we seek God's kingdom first that the other kingdoms of our life come into line.

Remember, those who seek their own promotion will lose it; and those who lose it for Christ's sake will find it.

TODAY I WILL...

☑ listen for God's guidance in every detail of my day

☑ live and work by the principles of His Word

☑ rejoice in the process as God molds me into His Son's image

LORD, YOU ARE OUR FATHER. WE ARE THE CLAY, AND YOU ARE THE POTTER. WE ARE ALL FORMED BY YOUR HAND.

ISAIAH 64:8 NLT

Isaiah and Jeremiah use the incredibly telling image of clay in the hand of the potter to convey to us the process through which God works with the broken and selfish vessels we are to "fix and mold us into vessels fit for the Master's use." (See Isaiah 64:8; Jeremiah 18:1-6; and 2 Timothy 2:21.) Broken or cracked pots are taken into the potter's hand and smashed and ground to powder. Then water is added to make them fresh clay again, and they are shaped and stretched anew to be formed into the image the designer desires. They are then fired in the tremendous heat of a kiln to be set permanently in the form the master desires so that no other forces can change or corrupt the vessel again. Not until the full process is completed does the master have a tool or vessel fit for his purposes and use; and the more important that use, the more time and attention to detail is taken in the process.

God is our potter and, as we all know, the process of becoming fit for His use is tough on us, the clay. It can be a painful, stretching, and difficult process as we are refined and molded into what God hopes we will be. The Bible tells us that we can be confident of one thing, "that He who has begun a good work in you will complete it until the day of Jesus Christ" (Philippians 1:6 NKJV). It also assures us, "We are God's masterpiece. He has created us anew in Christ Jesus, so that we can do the good things he planned for us long ago" (Ephesians 2:10 NLT).

Just as God delights in every detail of our lives, the only way to joyfully endure the process is to delight in every detail of our lives as well.

Remember, every detail of your life is in God's loving hands.

Today I Will...

- ☑ joyfully play my part in the orchestra of life around me

- ☑ play my part well and as instructed, whether or not I understand the "why" of my part

- ☑ measure my personal success by my team's success

How wonderful it is, how pleasant, for God's people to live together in harmony!

Psalm 133:1 tev

In a beautiful piece of music, every instrument has its part, and most don't even play the melody. Instead, each individual instrument builds the depth and quality of the piece by adding background harmonies and variations. There are places for some to play solos and other places where certain instruments rest and don't play at all. The key to success is the quality of each player doing exactly what his or her sheet music says to do, nothing more, nothing less. Working together in a business or church is not much different from performing a good piece of music.

One point that Jesus struggled continually to get across to His disciples is that living for Him is not about being the greatest or the best, but about serving sincerely while looking out for others as much as you look out for yourself. The disciples thus learned to overcome the temptation to promote themselves in order to contribute and celebrate in the growth of God's kingdom.

As you go about your day today, play your part with passion, enthusiasm, and wisdom—thus glorifying God in your every action. When we trust Him more than our own efforts to exalt and honor us, He never fails to respond to our faithfulness. Living in this manner may likely be the greatest song of praise and worship you ever offered your Father.

Remember, God won't be rewarding you for being a star, but for playing the part He has called you to unselfishly and with all of your heart.

TODAY I WILL...

☑ choose faith over worry

☑ turn my cares over to God in prayer and not take them back

☑ simply trust God in everything

CAN WORRY MAKE YOU

LIVE LONGER?

MATTHEW 6:27 CEV

The obvious answer to Jesus' question is "No, worry cannot make you live any longer. In fact, it seems to do just the opposite!"

It is interesting to think that worry—which is a form of stress—is on the list for chronic health risk factors alongside such things as improper diet, insufficient exercise, and smoking—all of which are self-control issues that living a biblical lifestyle addresses. Books now abound on the rediscovered value of avoiding the foods the Old Testament tells us to avoid and following the precepts of treating our bodies as the "temple of the Holy Spirit" (1 Corinthians 6:19). The Bible also tells us repeatedly not to worry. Who would have thought advice which seems so spiritual would also have physical benefits?

The fact is we have a long way to go before we will ever fathom the blessings of actually living according to the principles taught throughout the Bible. Learning how to live by faith in the positive rather than worrying over the negative is just one of them. Can you imagine the life we would live if we could apply them all? No wonder we hear so often, "God has a wonderful plan for your life."

Remember, worry is meditating on fear; faith comes from meditating on God's Word.

TODAY I WILL . . .

- ☑ believe the best
- ☑ see Christ in everyone I meet
- ☑ affirm greatness in others

"IF YOU GET RID OF UNFAIR PRACTICES, QUIT
BLAMING VICTIMS, QUIT GOSSIPING ABOUT OTHER
PEOPLE'S SINS . . . YOUR LIVES WILL BEGIN TO
GLOW IN THE DARKNESS, YOUR SHADOWED LIVES
WILL BE BATHED IN SUNLIGHT."

ISAIAH 58:9-10 MSG

All of us are natural critics. We have all felt compelled to analyze, pull apart, and point the finger. We are prone to examine, diagnose, and give our prognosis—our humble opinion—nobly offering "constructive criticism" out of genuinely heartfelt concern. Yet rather than trying to pinpoint the problem in others, we need to deliberately practice appreciating the divine we see in those around us, as well as ourselves, embracing the work of God's grace taking place in all who trust in it.

The philosopher Goethe put it this way: "Treat people as if they were what they ought to be, and help them to become what they are capable of being." We are reminded in 1 Corinthians 13:4-8 that this principle is what God's love is all about. Love does not find fault, but it focuses on the favorable. Love overlooks human weakness and magnifies the wonder of each human soul. Love covers a multitude of sins. (See 1 Peter 4:8 NIV.)

Lives can only be changed by the love of God. God's love overlooks wrongs, forgives, affirms, and appreciates the beauty and strength inherent in every person. In her groundbreaking book, *Leadership and the New Science,* Margaret Wheatley offers a quote by Eudora Welty summing up her intention to see beyond appearances: "My continuing passion is to part a curtain, that invisible shadow that falls between people, the veil of indifference to each other's presence, each other's wonder, each other's human plight."

Remember, every person is a miracle in process.

TODAY I WILL...

☑ be content

☑ give thanks and praise God for all things

☑ make a melody in my heart to the Lord

KEEP ON BEING FILLED WITH THE SPIRIT. THEN YOU WILL RECITE TO ONE ANOTHER PSALMS, HYMNS, AND SPIRITUAL SONGS. YOU WILL SING AND MAKE MUSIC TO THE LORD WITH YOUR HEARTS. YOU WILL ALWAYS GIVE THANKS TO GOD THE FATHER FOR EVERYTHING IN THE NAME OF OUR LORD JESUS CHRIST.

EPHESIANS 5:18-20 ISV

There is so much to be thankful for in our daily lives. We can choose to focus on what's wrong in people and the world at large, or we can take time to reflect on what's wonderful. When all else is said and done, at the end of the day it's the lives we've touched, the conversations we've taken part in, the things we've shared with others that determine our success and happiness.

Opportunities abound to content ourselves with a kind gesture, a gracious act, or a loving smile. It's in the sharing of joy that joy is found. Being thankful is the first step to sharing joy, and praising God by making melody in our hearts to the Lord stirs up that thankfulness. God requires so little of us that sometimes we forget the simplicity found in His peace and grace. Being thankful, content, and joyful is often the most profound witness we have to give, the best testimony we can offer, and the most effective way to honor and bring glory to God.

If we really believed that our purpose was to change the world with God's promise of eternal joy and infinite peace, we would indeed be joyful and at peace. As stated by author Peter Thigpen, of Executive Reserves, in *Encouraging the Heart:* "Really believe in your heart of hearts that your fundamental purpose, the reason for being, is to enlarge the lives of others. Your life will be enlarged also. And all of the other things we have been taught to concentrate on will take care of themselves."

Remember, our best weapon against strife and despair is the power of peace and joy.

Today I Will...

- ☑ pursue God
- ☑ be led by His Holy Spirit
- ☑ be mindful of His presence, knowing He is always with me

THE TRUE CHILDREN OF GOD ARE THOSE WHO LET
GOD'S SPIRIT LEAD THEM.

ROMANS 8:14 NCV

We know God loves us, for the Bible tells us so. We have been bought with a price. (See 1 Corinthians 6:20.) God created the entire universe to work out His plan of salvation, which includes you. It is indeed mind-boggling to think that God created the entire cosmos so you could take advantage of it. Before the dawn of time He knew you personally and planned a unique purpose for your life. For such a time as this were you created and brought to the earth. (See Esther 4:14.)

Meditating on God's purpose for all things—especially His unique purpose for you—will cause you to realign your priorities. Being mindful of why God has brought you into existence and how your life can contribute to His purpose and plan for all mankind will create a desire to dig into His Word, pursue His will, and press into His ways so you don't neglect the special assignment He has for you. Sometimes we feel we are falling short, not knowing exactly what God has called us to do. We stumble along desiring to fulfill God's great call on our lives but feel as though it is always eluding us. Of course, the only way to fully know our assignment, and to fulfill it, is to fully know God—allowing Him alone to fulfill us.

This is the simplicity found in Christ—to seek Him alone, His presence, His will. Every other fulfillment will follow. As long as we are seeking Him with our whole heart, pursing His truth with our entire mind, loving Him with all our strength, we will fulfill His greatest purpose on the earth and highest call upon our lives.

Remember, in His presence is fullness of joy. (See Psalm 16:11.)

TODAY I WILL...

- ☑ walk in the authority I have been given in Christ

- ☑ be a faithful steward of the truth I know

- ☑ choose faith over fear

"DO NOT BE AFRAID . . .
ONLY BELIEVE."

LUKE 8:50 NASB

Walking in the light of the truth we already possess can be more challenging than taking possession of truths we might not yet know. Often we are hearers only, not doers of the things we've been taught. We are like the man James spoke of who peers in the mirror yet forgets immediately upon turning away what he looks like. (See James 1:22-24.) We are told that we have been made the righteousness of God in Christ. We shout praises to God for redeeming us, restoring us, and making us new creatures in Christ. Yet we succumb daily to thoughts of inferiority, low self-esteem, or self-pity.

In warfare, the first steps to overcoming the enemy are to locate his position, understand his weapons, and be aware of his tactics. The enemy of our souls would have us believe that we are victims of circumstance—that there is nothing we can do to change our situation. Our enemy would have us believe that we are sitting ducks, vulnerable to whatever life throws our way.

Jesus told us the enemy comes only to kill, steal, and destroy—that he is the prince of lies and there is no truth in him (John 10:10; 8:44). We are warned that he roams the earth seeking whom he may devour (Peter 5:8). We are also told that God searches to and fro on the earth for those who would show themselves faithful. (See 2 Chronicles 16:9.) How do we show ourselves faithful? We remember who we are in Christ, that greater is He who is in us than he that is in the world (1 John 4:4). We remember that we have been given the name that is above every name (Philippians 2:9), that nothing is impossible for those who put their trust in God.

Remember, nothing is impossible for those who believe. (See Mark 9:23.)

Today I Will...

☑ enjoy the quiet and peace of focusing on accomplishing the tasks of my day

☑ pay more attention to what I have to do than what others "should be doing"

☑ speak only when truly necessary

This should be your ambition: to live a quiet life, minding your own business and working with your hands, just as we commanded you before. As a result, people who are not Christians will respect the way you live, and you will not need to depend on others to meet your financial needs.

1 Thessalonians 4:11-12 nlt

What do your work habits and conversation at the office communicate to others about God? Do you trust in office politicking for promotion more than doing good work and letting the truth speak for itself? Do you do things to draw attention to yourself to gain popularity? What is your real ambition as you walk through each day? Is it to get by doing as little as possible to earn your pay, or is your labor a sacrifice to God more than a means to getting one day closer to your next paycheck?

When Paul addressed the Thessalonians, he mentioned a couple of problems they were having with their communal living and providing for one another out of a common pool of resources. The largest of these seemed to be that while some worked hard for the benefit of all, others wasted the time they should have been working with idle talk and fussing about other people's business. Such people were actually stealing from the community, and Paul instructed that if they refused to work, they should not be fed. (See 2 Thessalonians 3:10.) To the church in Ephesus, he said, "Let him who stole steal no longer, but rather let him labor, working with his hands what is good, that he may have something to give him who has need" (Ephesians 4:28 NKJV). Their attitude was not to be sponging off of others, but always working hard so that they not only had enough to care for themselves on their own, but also had excess to give to those in need.

Work today ambitiously—and let that ambition be to please God and show trust in His provision more than anything else.

Remember, your actions —and work habits—speak louder than your words.

TODAY I WILL...

☑ keep God first in all things

☑ seek His kingdom before establishing my own

☑ let God lead me in my financial life as in all areas of my life

---

THE TITHE . . . IS THE LORD'S;

IT IS HOLY TO THE LORD.

LEVITICUS 27:30 NASB

The word tithe means "tenth." Many miss the fact that tithing is more than just giving a tenth of our income to the Lord. It is giving to God the first tenth of all revenue that comes through our hands. In this way we put God first in our finances, just as praying and praising God at the beginning of our day puts Him first in our planning and thinking. While some have argued that the tithe need not be a New Testament practice, those who do practice it today still realize the blessing of it given in Malachi 3:10 NKJV: "'Bring all the tithes into the storehouse, that there may be food in My house, and try Me now in this,' says the LORD of hosts, 'If I will not open for you the windows of heaven and pour out for you such blessing that there will not be room enough to receive it.'"

Obviously God's blessings are much more than money, but taking control of our relationship to money is crucial to our relationship with God. Jesus never stated that our choice on earth was between serving God or the devil, but rather serving God or material wealth. (See Matthew 6:24.) Because of this, tithing also holds an additional help: By giving the first ten percent of our income to God and not keeping it for ourselves, we master our money rather than letting it master us. And when we tithe and give off the top of our increase first, then we place it in service to God and His kingdom.

God's financial blessings will only make a positive impact in our lives when we have Jesus on the throne of our lives and not money or materialism.

Remember, when God blesses us, He adds no sorrow with it. (See Proverbs 10:22.)

TODAY I WILL...

☑ give to others as my heart dictates

☑ be a blessing to those who instruct me in God's Word

☑ be generous

EACH OF YOU MUST GIVE WHAT
YOU HAVE DECIDED IN YOUR HEART,
NOT WITH REGRET OR UNDER COMPULSION,
SINCE GOD LOVES A CHEERFUL GIVER.

2 CORINTHIANS 9:7 ISV

God likes to see His generosity reflected in His children, but this generosity cannot come from a home that is financially shaky and disorganized. There are many who are generous with their money and happy to be so, until their well dries up, cash grows tight, and their former generosity looks like foolishness because they have no money left. Although God never wants us to stop giving, giving is not His only concern. He not only wants us to tithe, He also expects us to take care of ourselves and our families with what He has given us.

While several places in the Bible tell us about the importance of giving to others with an open heart and the blessings that will result from such giving, we are also warned in 1 Timothy 5:8 NIV: "If anyone does not provide for his relatives, and especially for his immediate family, he has denied the faith and is worse than an unbeliever." God expects us not only to give to others as our hearts lead us, but also to set aside money to provide for the futures of our families. When we do both, we ensure that we will never regret the money we have given because we are responsible stewards with all God entrusted to us.

God loves cheerful, responsible generosity given out of a heart thankful for all God has blessed us with in our lives—including finances. The generosity of our giving does not make up for poor stewardship in other areas. However, diligent stewardship over all will likely make us joyful givers.

Remember, it was only the good stewards in the Parable of the Talents who entered into the joy of their Lord.

(See Matthew 25:13-30.)

TODAY I WILL...

☑ think corporately rather than just of my own advancement

☑ be a responsible teammate to both supervisors and those I supervise

☑ consider how my work provides for others and the growth of God's kingdom

"WHO, THEN, IS THE FAITHFUL AND WISE SERVANT WHOM HIS MASTER HAS PUT IN CHARGE OF HIS HOUSEHOLD TO GIVE THE OTHERS THEIR FOOD AT THE RIGHT TIME? HOW BLESSED IS THAT SERVANT WHOM HIS MASTER FINDS DOING THIS WHEN HE COMES!"

MATTHEW 24:45-46 ISV

When Jesus left the earth to go to the right hand of His Father in Heaven, He left us, His followers, as stewards of all He gave to us, in cooperation together as His Church. He literally left us as stewards over His household on the earth, expecting us to provide and care for one another.

As God's stewards on the earth, we make a mistake if we take too much ownership in this world. We are, after all, foreigners in a strange land hoping one day to live in God's eternal kingdom where our true citizenship lies. Yet we must live and operate here to work and provide for those in our households—and, Jesus added, to care for those who are hungry, thirsty, estranged, naked, sick, and in prison. (See Matthew 25:31-46.) Should our appointment as stewards of God's household until He returns change the motives that drive us forward in our work and how we acquire and manage the resources with which we have been entrusted?

As business leaders, we need to recognize not only the importance of what our businesses provide our customers, but also the security and provision our enterprises give to our employees and others through them. We must realize that if we manage our businesses so badly that others must be laid off, our company must cut back benefits in order to cover market changes, or we lose employees due to injuries or fatigue from overwork, we have failed in our stewardship with what God has entrusted to us. Good stewardship provides for others as well as their families; and God's Word is full of the wisdom necessary to help us do that.

Remember, God's Word has been given to us for success in every area of life.

TODAY I WILL...

☑ be patient

☑ be diligent

☑ plan for the long run more than for short-term gain

WEALTH [NOT EARNED BUT] WON IN HASTE OR UNJUSTLY OR FROM THE PRODUCTION OF THINGS FOR VAIN OR DETRIMENTAL USE [SUCH RICHES] WILL DWINDLE AWAY, BUT HE WHO GATHERS LITTLE BY LITTLE WILL INCREASE [HIS RICHES].

PROVERBS 13:11 AMP

Believe it or not, if you use it wisely, time is on your side. God does not tell us to be patient because He wants us to wait, but because time is always a component in His plans. He uses time to iron out the details He feels are important parts of our character development and success. He recognizes the destructive nature of sudden success to those who do not know His life-long purposes for them. Too often we think that sudden success justifies us. We do not realize that God's plans for our lives are much bigger and much more eternity-focused.

If we let financial success alone define our overall success in life, then we are letting wealth be our god rather than going to Jesus to mold us into His image. We do the same thing if we look at our bottom line and how little we make, concluding that we are failures. To make judgments based on wealth and profitability alone is to make money our lord and master more than Christ. To live by Jesus' standards above all, however, is to make money a servant and tool for us to accomplish His goals and purposes. As the Bible tells us: "The blessing of the Lord makes a person rich, and he adds no sorrow with it" (Proverbs 10:22 NLT) and "Unless the LORD builds the house, they labor in vain who build it" (Psalm 127:1 NASB).

God does want us to prosper in all areas of our lives, but not at the expense of true lasting prosperity and peace.

Remember, God's ways are higher —and more lasting—than ours.

Today I Will...

☑ live as God directs because I trust Him

☑ let God's desires fill my heart

☑ be a person of my word just as God is of His Word

Trust the LORD and live right! The land will be yours, and you will be safe. Do what the LORD wants, and he will give you your heart's desire.

Psalm 37:3-4 CEV

The fundamental battle in the human heart is whether to trust God or ourselves. As we learn of God's ways and read His Word, we are commonly expected to obey before we understand—something that is very contrary to our human nature. In fact, in our modern society, we commonly fault leadership for our lack of support, not because they are wrong, but because we don't understand their visions enough to plug into them. We often feel that our rebellious nature against authority is justifiable because leaders have failed to inspire us to obedience.

While we should certainly strive to understand, we cannot let our lack of understanding justify disobedience to God's ways. Often doing such things as keeping our promises to the point that they hurt us (Psalm 15:4) or promoting the interests of truth over our own interests (1 Corinthians 13:6) seems foolish in the short-term while, in fact, these actions are the very things that build our long-term and eternal success. It may seem odd to think that the quickest way to achieve our heart's desire is to follow God rather than to directly pursue those desires, but that is exactly the promise God has given us in His Word. Do we trust His Word enough to follow His promises more than our own understanding?

Remember, true security —financial or otherwise—can come only from God.

TODAY I WILL...

☑ show my love for God in word and deed

☑ show my love for God in how I treat others

☑ be satisfied with His blessings

WHOEVER LOVES MONEY NEVER HAS MONEY ENOUGH; WHOEVER LOVES WEALTH IS NEVER SATISFIED WITH HIS INCOME. THIS TOO IS MEANINGLESS. AS GOODS INCREASE, SO DO THOSE WHO CONSUME THEM. AND WHAT BENEFIT ARE THEY TO THE OWNER EXCEPT TO FEAST HIS EYES ON THEM?

ECCLESIASTES 5:10-11 NIV

The love of money could have no power in our lives except for its power to deceive. Often the more power it has over us, the less power we believe it has over us. Just as many who have a good deal of wealth feel that they control it more than it controls them, so many who have little assume that money has no control over them because they have so little of it. Yet, at the same time, the pursuit of money determines when they get up in the morning, how they spend their time, how much time they have to pray or serve God in their churches or community, and almost everything else they do, or don't do, in their lives. If we are more concerned with our checking account balance than whether God is leading us to do or give something, what is truly our master—God or money?

Most of us think that if we just make more money, then we will get a better handle on our finances, but the opposite is actually true. Unless we get control of our spending when we have only a little, we will never get control of it when we have more. And unless we control money, it will control us. Many look to their next raise as the answer to their financial problems only to discover that six months after their raise they are worse off than before. The only answer is to apply God's wisdom and self-control to our relationship with money now, so we can establish our freedom from money in the future. It does not work the other way around.

Remember, true riches
come from obeying God
above everything else.

Today I Will...

☑ be trustworthy

☑ work to learn

☑ use what I know and have to be a blessing to others

"To those who use well what they are given, even more will be given. But from those who are unfaithful, even what little they have will be taken away."

Luke 19:26 nlt

How much can God trust you? If He gave you something great to manage for Him, what would you do with it? Whose kingdom would you build—yours or His?

The fact of the matter is, whatever we have has been given to us by God to manage for the benefit of those around us—whether it be the time that we have, the money and wealth we have control over, or the gifts and talents He has given us. The condition of our hearts towards God will determine what we do with these things. As St. Ambrose once said, "Just as riches are an impediment to virtue in the wicked, so in the good they are an aid of virtue." Do you want God to be able to trust you with more? Then you need to become more trustworthy.

The parable of the talents tells us that God has trusted us to multiply what He has given us while He is gone from the earth. Other scriptures tell us that the teaching of the Bible and God's Holy Spirit have been given us to help us use our resources wisely. What excuse have we then to do anything less than increase what we have been given so His kingdom on earth might increase in the process?

Remember, God will call for an accounting of our stewardship.

TODAY I WILL...

☑ be the person God made me to be

☑ be transparent before God and myself

☑ let my lifestyle be an offering of praise to God

"IT'S WHO YOU ARE AND THE WAY YOU LIVE THAT
COUNT BEFORE GOD. YOUR WORSHIP MUST ENGAGE
YOUR SPIRIT IN THE PURSUIT OF TRUTH. THAT'S
THE KIND OF PEOPLE THE FATHER IS OUT LOOKING
FOR: THOSE WHO ARE SIMPLY AND HONESTLY
THEMSELVES BEFORE HIM IN THEIR WORSHIP."

JOHN 4:23 MSG

How we live worships God. Too many identify praise and worship as something we do in church services. And many people identify it as the portion of the service that comes just before the offering and pastor's message. However, how we engage ourselves during the entire service is our praise and worship—as well as how we conduct ourselves the rest of the week.

Living a lifestyle of praise and worship is also our only way to avoid being self-deceived. We should pray every morning as David prayed in Psalm 139:23-24 MSG: "Investigate my life, O God, find out everything about me; cross-examine and test me, get a clear picture of what I'm about; see for yourself whether I've done anything wrong—then guide me on the road to eternal life." Only by standing transparent before God can we walk without self-deception.

Living a sincere life before God and others is also the greatest form of worship we can offer God. As the old saying goes, "Imitation is the sincerest form of flattery," and trying to live like Jesus is exactly what pleases God.

Remember, who you are and what you do will always worship louder than how you sing on Sunday mornings.

TODAY I WILL...

☑ take time for others

☑ cut down on unimportant busyness

☑ live today to learn how to love God and others more completely

---

"'LOVE THE LORD YOUR GOD. . . . LOVE OTHERS AS WELL AS YOU LOVE YOURSELF.' . . . THESE TWO COMMANDS ARE PEGS; EVERYTHING IN GOD'S LAW AND THE PROPHETS HANGS FROM THEM."

MATTHEW 22:37-40 MSG

Too often we lose the real purpose of living life in the tasks that consume our time. We lose what is important for the sake of what shouts the loudest for our attention. As Pastor Rick Warren has said, "Busyness is the enemy of relationships. We become preoccupied with making a living, doing our work, paying bills, and accomplishing goals as if these tasks are the point of life. They are not. The point of life is learning to love—God and people."[5]

It takes real discipline to look into the face of a shouting, urgent demand and say, "No, not right now—I have to go spend time with someone." We assume that that time, unless it has a specific task attached, can wait. Yet as it has often been said, "love"—especially for children—is spelled "t-i-m-e." Perhaps in planning our days we should allot time to those we are consciously trying to love rather than letting relationships slide by for our urgent "to do's." It is, after all, okay to love what we do at work, just not more than our families or God.

To be successful in business today, we are commonly required to spend more than the minimum of forty hours a week in the office getting things done. But how much of that time is really spent getting important things done rather than getting caught up in time-wasters or being inefficient in our work during the regular work hours? Perhaps we should ask ourselves "Is this really the way I want to spend my love?"

Remember, what we trade our time for is what becomes most important to us.

TODAY I WILL...

☑ pray

☑ take time to listen for God's direction throughout the day

☑ spend time with God

VERY EARLY IN THE MORNING,
WHILE IT WAS STILL DARK, JESUS GOT UP,
LEFT THE HOUSE AND WENT OFF TO A SOLITARY
PLACE, WHERE HE PRAYED.

MARK 1:35 NIV

Where do you get the strength that you need to live each day? If Jesus needed to get up each morning and pray in order to live God's purposes for His life on this earth, how much more do we need to get up and pray to live the lives God has called us to live?

In the busyness of life, taking time to pray a few minutes each day—let alone spending a half-hour or hour in prayer each day—seems impossible to do. Yet how many of us unconsciously spend more than an hour each day watching television, listening to the radio or a new CD, and talking on the phone? Since we gladly spend that time in such insignificant pursuits, why do we consider it a waste to spend the same amount of time with the CEO of the universe?

In Revelation 3:20 NASB, Jesus declares, "I stand at the door and knock; if anyone hears My voice and opens the door, I will come in to him and will dine with him, and he with Me." Are we willing enough to believe this promise that we start blocking out time to spend with God each day? If Jesus needed such time with His Father, can we truly expect to succeed in our missions in life without spending at least as much time with Him?

Remember, God created us to have fellowship and relationship with Him.

TODAY I WILL...

☑ seek to help others discover and fulfill their God-given purposes

☑ consider whose help I will need as I seek to fulfill my God-given purposes

☑ strengthen the quality of my relationships

IF ONE PART HURTS, EVERY OTHER PART IS INVOLVED IN THE HURT, AND IN THE HEALING. IF ONE PART FLOURISHES, EVERY OTHER PART ENTERS INTO THE EXUBERANCE.

1 CORINTHIANS 12:26 MSG

Paul used the example of the human body to illustrate the nature of our relationships to one another under the headship of Jesus. His point was that as a body, though we are many separate parts distinguishable from one another in function and appearance, we need one another to accomplish anything of significance. The mouth would struggle to eat without the hands, and the hands would be aimless in searching for food if the eyes did not direct them. All of these parts would fail in a short time if the mouth could not take in the food and digest it to give nourishment to all of the parts. In this way we not only work together but also need each other to survive.

Jesus' example shows us that for the body to operate correctly, we must live our lives for each other rather than ourselves. Jesus not only gave His life on the cross, but He also spent His entire ministry meeting the needs of others, whether it was a healing touch, a better understanding of the nature of His Father, or a stern rebuke to shake them from self-delusion and pride. As 1 John 3:16 MSG says: "Christ sacrificed his life for us. This is why we ought to live sacrificially for our fellow believers, and not just be out for ourselves." Romans 12:1 also tells us to be living sacrifices—not to deny our lives and die for others necessarily, but to have the courage to live in the pursuit of helping others fulfill God's best plan for their lives.

The most successful and long-standing businesses are those that see the needs of others and find ways to solve them. Similarly, there is no more successful employee than the one who is willing to reach out and help others in need.

Remember, we are members
of one body in Christ.

TODAY I WILL...

☑ carefully consider my actions and words

☑ trust God's timing

☑ recognize there is a time to be patient and wait

THERE'S AN OPPORTUNE TIME TO DO THINGS, A RIGHT TIME FOR EVERYTHING ON THE EARTH.

ECCLESIASTES 3:1 MSG

Living in the instant society of today—where quality and value are often traded for speed of delivery—patience seems a lost virtue. Yet as much today as ever, releasing products or services at the right time rather than too early or too late can still make or break a business venture. Old businesses that fail to change or respond correctly to the needs and operating models of the day often find themselves lapped by their more responsive competitors. While doing things more quickly and efficiently for others is increasingly important today, the value of waiting for the right time to release a new product or taking the time to do a job thoroughly are still crucial to success.

As Christians, we need to remember to be patient—plugging into God's timing rather than always insisting on our own. The only way to live in this manner is to continually seek His counsel and dedicate all of our ways and dreams to Him daily. God knows the best time for anything much better than we do—which, of course, means that we will need to wait patiently for certain things. At other times we will need to put aside what we think is more important to do something He has put on our hearts. Sometimes we must follow His voice to do things we don't think we are ready to do.

The power of patience is to trust God's timing in all things and obey promptly when He calls upon us, even when it doesn't make any sense. Patience is doing things well and completely in a world warped by "instant access" and "next-day delivery." Doing the right thing often depends on when as much as what, so let God guide you into His perfect timing in whatever you are praying for today.

Remember, God always knows
the best time for anything.

TODAY I WILL...

☑ cherish inspiration

☑ schedule blocks of undisturbed time for creativity

☑ guard what I allow into my mind and heart

WATCH OVER YOUR HEART WITH ALL DILIGENCE,
FOR FROM IT FLOW THE SPRINGS OF LIFE.

PROVERBS 4:23 NASB

The most common way that God leads us is through our conscience, which is the voice of our heart or human spirit. As our body connects with and touches the physical world with our five senses, so our born-again spirit touches the realm of God—the spiritual world. The divine quality of our life flows from God's realm into our world—which is why we pray that His will be done on earth just as it is in heaven. (See Matthew 6:10.) But there are three main things that choke back the seeds of God's wisdom sown in our hearts that are trying to produce good things in our lives: "the cares of this world, the deceitfulness of riches, and the desires for other things." (See Mark 4:19 AMP.)

We don't miss hearing God's voice because He is not speaking, but because our minds are clogged with other things. We are caught up with the demands of the day or moment; we are daydreaming of what it will be like when we are thin enough or finally make enough money to have everything we want; we are thinking of the new things we want to buy with our next paycheck or raise; or we are rolling over and over in our thoughts the images of the movie or TV show we watched the night before. We get so earthly minded we are of no heavenly good.

We are designed to live by God's inspiration to us—as He speaks to our hearts the direction and creative ideas we need to fulfill His purposes. Take time this week to weed out the junk and distractions in your mind and find quality, quiet times to listen for His voice.

Remember, God always has something worthwhile to tell you.

TODAY I WILL...

- ☑ esteem learning new things more than making more money

- ☑ value wisdom over knowledge or desire

- ☑ do what is right according to wisdom, not want

GET WISDOM—IT'S WORTH MORE THAN MONEY;
CHOOSE INSIGHT OVER INCOME EVERY TIME.

PROVERBS 16:16 MSG

In his best-selling book, *Rich Dad, Poor Dad*, author Richard Kiyosaki passes on the wisdom of his "rich dad"—to work to learn rather than working for a paycheck. In the same way, Solomon advises us that wisdom is more valuable than riches and gold, because such things can easily pass away if we are foolish. But if we are wise, we can always methodically apply that wisdom to establish financial security time and again. As he advises elsewhere in Proverbs, those who seek wealth may achieve it but lose other things in the process, while those who seek wisdom find that it brings a long, satisfied life on one hand and riches and honor on the other. (See Proverbs 3:16.) Riches and honor follow wisdom, not the other way around.

While knowledge of how to do things is important, wisdom is more valuable. While knowledge is defined as learning information and processes, wisdom is the ability to know when and how to correctly apply that knowledge. Knowledge tells us what to do, while wisdom supplies the when, where, how, and why of our actions. One works to earn a paycheck, the other to fulfill God-given dreams.

God is calling His children to more than just working for a living. Good, satisfying work is part of His promise to us, and that means that whatever we do will not just meet our financial needs, but also fulfill our heart's desires. God has more than a job for you; He has a mission for you to fulfill, and He has given you what you need to realize that mission in the wisdom of the Bible. Pledge to live by it today.

Remember, God knows.

TODAY I WILL...

☑ be great in service to others

☑ seek to earnestly understand
the needs of those around me

☑ lead by example and attitude

THE GREATEST AMONG YOU
MUST BE A SERVANT.

MATTHEW 23:11 NLT

Servant Leadership has been in the headlines, on book covers, and a buzz word in management circles for many years. The concept is not new, but revelation of its power to inspire change is relatively recent. Of course, Jesus defined servant leadership in a myriad of ways. He laid the groundwork and set the standard for what it means to be a true servant leader. Ever since Jesus walked the earth, people have aspired to emulate His method of leadership.

Servant leadership requires one to put aside self-interest. A true leader does not self-promote, but promotes others. Christ-like leaders understand that they must lay down their lives for the good of the whole; they remember that only by helping others to succeed will they truly find their own success. True leadership requires one to put service before self-gratification—sacrifice before significance.

Responsibility is determined by a leader's ability to respond. Responsible leaders are responsive leaders. Richard Leider says it this way: "It doesn't take a degree in psychology to help people help themselves. It requires a leadership art with people that makes them feel heard. It requires 'that soft stuff'—your heart. The word heart is made up of two words: hear and art. The core of the change process is the art of hearing. Listening is absolutely essential to change."[6]

Remember, Jesus was responsive. Jesus was never too busy to listen, too distracted to hear, or too tired to respond.

TODAY I WILL...

☑ savor every moment

☑ look for God at work in every detail

☑ remember why I was created

WHEN I CONSIDER YOUR HEAVENS, THE WORK OF
YOUR FINGERS, THE MOON AND THE STARS,
WHICH YOU HAVE SET IN PLACE, WHAT IS MAN
THAT YOU ARE MINDFUL OF HIM,
THE SON OF MAN THAT YOU CARE FOR HIM?

PSALM 8:3-4 NIV

Sometimes it is easy to forget that God is at work in every situation, every detail, every person. If we stop to look, we will see His workmanship. If we stop to sense Him, we will feel Him near. The whole earth is filled with His wonder. David could hardly find words enough to express his awe for the Lord's handiwork. From the splendor of the solar system to the miraculous workings of each cell, from the brilliant colors of a sunrise to the majesty of the highest mountains—God is at work in all.

We can see the nature of God in nature itself. The beauty, majesty, serenity, splendor—it is all there for us to see if we will look. God speaks to us through His creation. Psalm 1:3 immediately directs us to the trees and rivers; "firmly planted like a tree by the river giving forth its fruit in season." Jesus taught of being fruitful branches abiding in the vine (John 15:5). The Spirit of God is likened to rivers of living water that fail not. (See John 7:38-39.) Yes, the earth is filled with His glory!

Pay attention to the beauty surrounding you. Tune your senses to the glory of the Lord filling the earth. Give heed to the wonder and magnificence of God's creation. God can be seen in everything, because all things came from God. "Taste and see that the Lord is good" (Psalm 34:8 NIV). Look around at all creation, every creature. Praise the Lord with every breath, in every moment, because if you incline your senses, you can sense God in everything.

Remember, creation reflects its Creator.

Today I Will...

- ☑ delight in others
- ☑ be a healing and helping balm to those around me
- ☑ recognize the community in my workplace as we function together

There are many of us, but we each
are part of the body of Christ,
as well as part of one another.

Romans 12:5 cev

At the funeral of former president Ronald Reagan, Supreme Court Justice Sandra Day O'Connor read from a sermon delivered by John Winthrop in 1630: "We must delight in each other, make others' conditions our own; rejoice together, mourn together, labor and suffer together . . . always having before our eyes our commission and community in the work, as members of the same body. . . . For we must consider that we shall be as a city upon a hill. . . . The eyes of all people are upon us."

Not only must we continually remind ourselves that we are members of the same body, all striving to achieve the same goals in Christ, but that we are each a "city upon a hill" with the eyes of all people upon us. The apostle John said that others would know we are saved because of our love for each other. (See John 13:35.) We are told by Paul in Romans 12:15 NIV to rejoice with those who rejoice and to mourn with those who mourn. How can we walk in the unity of peace if we don't carry each other's burdens?

We can see how the principles of sowing and reaping come into play regarding our compassion for others. As with so many other areas of life, the measure we use will determine how all will be measured back to us. (See Luke 6:38.) If we seek peace, we must show peace. If we want to be blessed, we must be a blessing. If we desire mercy, we must demonstrate mercy. "Whoever stops his ears at the cry of the poor will cry out himself and not be heard" (Proverbs 21:13 AMP).

Remember, your success is determined by the degree to which you help others succeed.

TODAY I WILL...

☑ stay connected

☑ look for opportunities to generate strength to the weaknesses of others

☑ choose compassion over criticism

LOVE NEVER GIVES UP.

1 CORINTHIANS 13:4 MSG

Leadership speaker and trainer Tim Redmond talks about the importance of staying connected. He sheds new light on the opportunities presented by each interaction we experience as leaders. Connectedness is important not only to sharing one another's strengths, but also to healing one another's weaknesses. Redmond states, "the test of our leadership, the mark of our maturity, the strength of our heart are all measured by how we respond to the 'weaknesses' of other people. Are we controlled by them, or do these 'weaknesses' provide an avenue to exercise the healing, connecting strength of our leadership?"[7]

Redmond goes on to say "your greatness—your purpose for living—involves bringing strength to the weaknesses of others. Your leadership is attracted to chaos. Your greatness released brings lasting order to that chaos. The big Leadership Test is a test of direction. When confronted with frustrations, anger, or any negative emotion that arises from your interactions with others, do you look 'outward' to judge, accuse, and blame; or do you go 'inward' to respond from your healing strength?"[8]

As a leader, you are required to consistently demonstrate a response of peace and healing instead of discord and friction. You are the fulcrum that determines the course your organization will ultimately take. The seemingly small, inconsequential decisions you make each day in choosing peace over pride will determine whether you stay connected to the true Source of all power and grace.

Remember, your daily connections can be a powerful source of strength and healing.

TODAY I WILL...

☑ practice being still

☑ rest in the knowledge of God

☑ let the peace of God rule in my heart and mind

SURRENDER YOUR WHOLE BEING TO HIM TO BE
USED FOR RIGHTEOUS PURPOSES.

ROMANS 6:13 TEV

For years monks have practiced the art of "centering prayer" or "contemplative prayer." Thomas Keating, a Trappist monk, widely read author, and founder of the organization Contemplative Outreach, defines contemplative prayer as "The opening of mind and heart, our whole being, to God, the Ultimate Mystery, beyond thoughts, words, and emotions. It is a process of interior purification that leads, if we consent, to divine union."

Another well-known author and Trappist monk, Thomas Merton, taught that the spiritual search takes us deeply inward, toward the Christ hidden within each of us. He believes we meet this Christ in solitude and contemplation. But such a life is not the special prerogative of the monk; every Christian is called to it. God is everywhere to be experienced by anyone at any given time—any time, that is, we are able to quiet our minds enough to be mindful of God's presence. Merton put it this way, "Life is very simple: we are living in a world that is absolutely transparent to God, and God is shining through it all the time. This is not a fable or a nice story. It is true. God manifests himself everywhere, in every thing, in people and in things and in nature and in events. You cannot be without God. It's impossible. Simply impossible."

Jesus said to enter our inner room, close the door, and pray in secret. (See Matthew 6:6.) He told the disciples to "come away by yourselves to a deserted place, and rest a while" (Mark 6:31 AMP). To hear God we must be quiet, to sense Him we must be still, and to see Him sometimes we must look within ourselves.

Remember, God is always present—both in our world and in us.

GOD'S TO BE LISTS

The Beatitudes
Matthew 5:3-12

The Fruit of the Spirit
Galatians 5:22-23

God's Love
1 Corinthians 13:4-8

ENDNOTES

1. Rick Warren, *The Purpose-Driven Life: What On Earth Am I Here For?* (Grand Rapids, Michigan: Zondervan, 2002), 46.

2. David Michael Levin, *The Listening Self* (New York: Routledge, 1989), 119.

3. James M. Kouzes and Barry Z. Posner, *The Leadership Challenge* (New York: Jossey-Bass, 1996), 398, 399.

4. Ibid.

5. Rick Warren, *The Purpose-Driven Life: What On Earth Am I Here For?* (Grand Rapids, Michigan: Zondervan, 2002), 125.

6. Richard Leider, "The Ultimate Leadership Challenge: Self-Leadership" *Leader of the Future*, (New York: Jossey-Bass, 1996), 290.

7. Tim Redmond, *Leadership Insights*, July 2004, Redmond Leadership Institute.

8. Ibid.

Additional copies of this book are available
from your local bookstore.

If you have enjoyed this book,
or if it has impacted your life,
we would like to hear from you.

Please contact us at:

Honor Books,
An Imprint of Cook Communications Ministries
4050 Lee Vance View
Colorado Springs, CO 80918

Or through our website:

www.cookministries.org